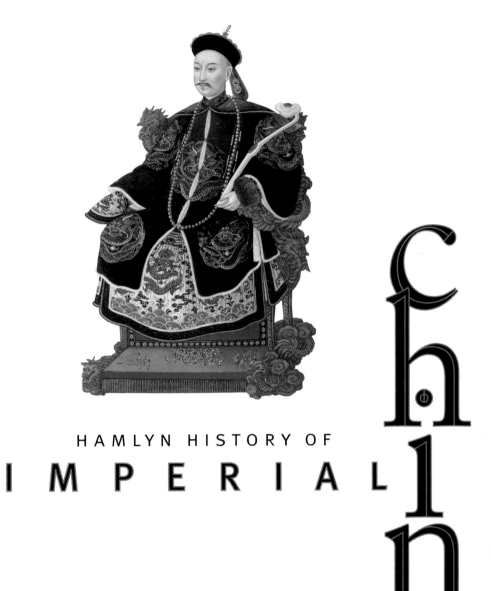

HAMLYN HISTORY OF
IMPERIAL CHINA

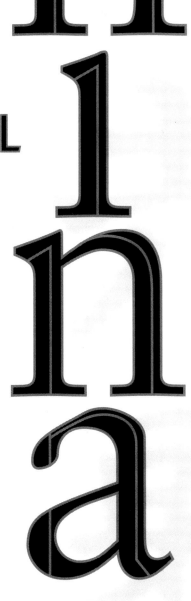

HAMLYN HISTORY OF
IMPERIAL

NATHANIEL HARRIS

HAMLYN

Publishing Director: Laura Bamford
Executive Editor: Julian Brown
Senior Editor: Trevor Davies
Art Director: Keith Martin
Executive Art Editor: Mark Stevens
Design: Les Needham
Picture Research: Wendy Gay
Production Controller: Clare Smedley

First published in Great Britain in 1999
by Hamlyn, an imprint of
Octopus Publishing Group Limited
2-4 Heron Quays,
London E14 4JP

ISBN 0 600 59422 X

A catalogue record for this book is available
from the British Library

Produced by Toppan
Printed in China

CONTENTS

INTRODUCTION

CHINESE CIVILIZATION WAS ONE OF HUMANITY'S MOST ASTONISHING ACHIEVEMENTS. IT ENDURED FOR MUCH LONGER THAN THE SEEMINGLY ETERNAL CIVILIZATION OF ANCIENT EGYPT, AND IT EMBRACED MORE TERRITORY AND A LARGER POPULATION THAN ANY PRE-MODERN EMPIRE OR CULTURE. ITS WAY OF LIFE BECAME THE CULTURAL STANDARD FOR THE ENTIRE FAR EAST FROM THAILAND TO JAPAN. ITS ARTS AND INVENTIONS CHANGED THE WORLD. THOUGH REMOTE FROM OTHER ADVANCED SOCIETIES, CHINA DID RECEIVE IDEAS AND TECHNIQUES FROM THE OUTSIDE WORLD; BUT ITS RELATIVE ISOLATION MEANT THAT THESE COULD BE ADAPTED AND ABSORBED INTO A SOCIETY THAT NEVER LOST ITS DISTINCTIVE CHARACTER WHILE EMPERORS SAT ON THE DRAGON THRONE, AND IN SOME IMPORTANT RESPECTS EVEN SURVIVED THE END OF THE EMPIRE IN 1912.

This is not to say that Chinese civilization was static, although it is true that the Chinese themselves venerated tradition and believed that doing so would bring order and stability in a dangerous world. Some typical features of their culture such as semi-divine rulers and ancestor-worship were present from the very beginning of the historical record. But it was not until 1,500 years later that Confucius began his life work in a still-divided China, creating the enduring ideal of the Superior Man: benevolent, affable and self-controlled (and consequently 'inscrutable' in western eyes), he was a dutiful son and servant of the state, roles eventually combined in a unique fashion with those of the gifted amateur artist and writer.

The empire itself was founded only in the 3rd century BC, in an area of North China that would come to look quite small by comparison with its final extent. The First Emperor built the famous Great Wall as a barrier against the northern steppe peoples who troubled Imperial China throughout its history. Another vital element in Chinese culture, the Buddhist religion, was imported from India in the early centuries AD. And one of the empire's most remarkable innovations, the civil service entrance examination, took centuries to establish and only reached its mature form under the Song dynasty (960–1279), heralding the emergence of the Confucian scholar-officials as China's ruling class. Similarly, while the visual and tactile arts in lacquer and jade were of great antiquity, porcelain – along with tea, China's most famous product – seems to have originated in the 8th century and also reached its apogee under the Song.

In fact it was only by the 13th century that the elements generally regarded as typical of imperial China had all come into being. Ironically, this was the century in which all of China was conquered for the first time by outsiders, the Mongols. When the Venetian merchant-traveller Marco Polo reached China in the 1270s, he was received by a Mongol emperor, Kublai Khan, who was just completing the conquest of the country; but the sophisticated city life that the visitor subsequently admired at Beijing, Hangzhou and Yangzhou was essentially the creation of the native Chinese. Polo's awe-struck descriptions are a reminder of the advanced character of Chinese society over the centuries. The empire that had traded silk with the Romans, that had discovered gunpowder, printing, paper and the compass, was still ahead of Europe in Polo's time. It would not be decisively overtaken until the 19th century, when the imperial government failed to grasp the scale of the challenge from a now technologically superior West, and a series of defeats and humiliations led to the downfall of the old order.

Since the Chinese do not use our Latin alphabet, there are different ways of transliterating Chinese words. In this book the modern pinyin system has been preferred, giving Beijing rather than the older Peking, and Qin rather than Ch'in. One or two familiar names (Canton, Shanghai) have been retained, and in a few instances the older form has been given in parentheses after the pinyin version. Depending on the period in which they reigned, Chinese emperors have been variously known by a personal name, a posthumous title or a reign-title; for simplicity these distinctions have been ignored and the terms have all been used as though they were personal names.

'Horse and Groom in Winter', painting by Zhao Mengfu (1254–1322); a lovely example of the Chinese artist's fluent linear style and insight into animals and the natural world.

1 THE MIDDLE KINGDOM

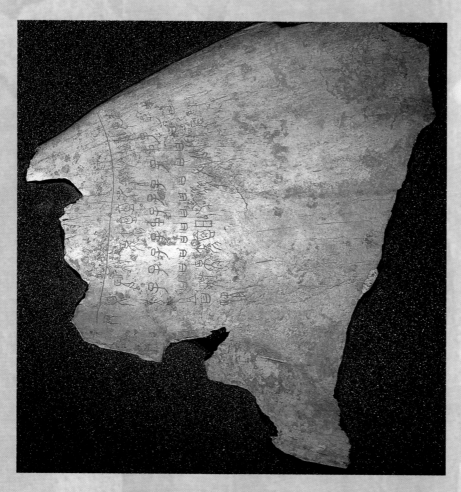

THERE WERE FLOURISHING HUMAN SETTLEMENTS IN MANY PARTS OF CHINA BY 2000 BC, BUT THE NUCLEUS OF THE FUTURE CHINESE STATE WAS FORMED IN THE NORTH, ALONG THE VALLEY OF THE YELLOW RIVER. SEMI-DIVINE KINGS REIGNED AND STATES CAME AND WENT FOR CENTURIES BEFORE THE FIRST EMPIRE WAS CREATED IN 221 BC BY SHI HUANGDI OF QIN (CH'IN), WHICH GAVE ITS NAME TO CHINA. RULED FROM THE DRAGON THRONE BY THE SON OF HEAVEN, THE CELESTIAL EMPIRE BECAME A BEACON OF CIVILIZATION, DAZZLING ITS NEIGHBOURS AND CONVERTING THEM TO THE CHINESE WAY OF LIFE EVEN DURING PERIODS WHEN ITS SOIL WAS OVERRUN BY FIERCE STEPPE PEOPLES. UNDERSTANDABLY THE CHINESE REGARDED THEIR LAND AS THE MIDDLE KINGDOM (THAT IS, THE CENTRE OF THE WORLD) AND ACCEPTED PHILOSOPHICALLY THE CYCLICAL RISE AND FALL OF DYNASTIES, EACH UPHEAVAL SIGNIFYING THAT THE MANDATE OF HEAVEN (DIVINE APPOINTMENT TO RULE) WAS PASSING FROM ONE HOUSE TO ANOTHER.

EARLY CHINA

Long before the birth of Imperial China, small bands of near-humans, or hominids, lived in East Asia, hunting or gathering available foods and using primitive stone tools. One hominid type became famous in the 1920s as Peking Man, when remains of a group were found in caves near the modern capital, Beijing (Peking). Since then there have been many finds, both of the earlier hominids and of humans of the modern type, who are thought to have lived in China at least 80,000 years ago.

The next great phase of prehistory, the Neolithic (New Stone Age), can be more directly linked with the development of China's distinctive civilization. During the Neolithic, humans learned to grow crops and domesticate animals; consequently they settled down and lived in stable communities, where they developed skills such as pottery-making and weaving. All advanced societies have passed through a Neolithic phase, but at very different times and basing themselves on very different crops. Neolithic settlements in China date back to about

7000 BC and became widespread by about 5000 BC. They sprang up independently in a number of different areas, including the lower Yangtze River, the middle Yellow River (Huang Ho) and the south-east coast. This is not really surprising in view of China's near-continental size, which encompassed a great variety of geographical features and climatic conditions. One division, between North and South, played a crucial role in Chinese history and became apparent at a very early date. In the cool, dry North, millet was the staple crop; the region was inherently vulnerable, with steppes and forests even further north from which fierce nomads were likely to erupt. By contrast, the wet and warm South was the potentially wealthy rice-bowl of China, encouraging a more relaxed (and sometimes decadent) way of life.

Several Neolithic and later cultures contributed to the shaping of Chinese civilization. But the nucleus of the Chinese state was formed on the North China Plain, in the middle Yellow River valley, where the great Yellow River met the River Wei and abruptly changed direction to flow east. The first known dynasty in the region, the shadowy Xia, probably reigned between about 2000 BC and 1750 BC. No indisputable evidence has been found to prove that it even existed, but it appears in the records compiled by much later but very reliable Chinese historians such as Sima Qian (c. 145–c. 86 BC), the accuracy

Opposite page: an oracle bone dating from the 2nd millennium BC. Such bones were used to prophesy the future; questions and answers scratched on them include the earliest known Chinese writing.

Left: ritual cooking vessel from the Shang period (c.1750–1127 BC) with stylized dragon mask decoration. Shang bronzes are among the greatest of China's artistic achievements.

Below: Shang bronze vessel. These strange, beautiful objects were not made for everyday purposes, but were used for offerings to the ancestors. They have survived because they were generally buried with their owners.

Right: Shang ceremonial bronze axe. The Shang kings seem to have been semi-divine beings; like the pharaohs of ancient Egypt, they lived by ritual and ruled over a rigidly hierarchical society.

Far right: coin from the Warring States (464–222 BC) or subsequent Han period. Preceded by shells, bars of iron and other objects, the first coins were minted in China around the 7th century BC.

Ritual mystery and the power to foretell the future no doubt helped to raise the king and nobility far above the common people. They were even physically segregated at times, since great Shang cities such as Anyang and Zhengzhou consisted of palace-temples protected by thick walls and surrounded – but at a distance – by villages of

of whose king-lists for the subsequent Shang dynasty have been confirmed by archaeological finds in recent times.

The existence of the Shang dynasty (c. 1750–1027 BC) was also questioned until excavations in the 1920s uncovered written and material proofs of its existence. These also illustrated the extent to which the Shang state had its roots in the past, although it operated on a vastly greater scale. Neolithic cultures had developed some form of class or caste system, and constructed defensive enclosures; and bronze working began around 2000 BC, in the late Neolithic or the Xia period. In most civilizations the Bronze Age has been associated with god-kings, human sacrifice, gigantic building projects and military prowess; and much the same pattern prevailed during the Shang period. The king was not only a hunter and warrior, but also the intermediary between heaven and earth. Every few days he consulted his ancestors by a form of divination. 'Oracle bones' were heated, and the cracks that appeared on them were interpreted as the answers to questions about forthcoming events and future prospects; the questions and answers, written on the bones, are the earliest certain examples of Chinese writing (c. 1400 BC). Shorter inscriptions appear a little later on some of the magnificent ritual bronzes for which the Shang period is famous; they were used to honour the ancestors, and were owned by, and subsequently buried with, Shang magnates.

artisans and other workers. Even more striking is the evidence of human sacrifices, sometimes numbering hundreds. The victims have been discovered in foundations (presumably consecrating walls or a building) and also in the dozen or so grand royal tombs at Anyang, the last Shang capital. As well as servants and captives, the tombs contained entire chariots with their horses and drivers; and enough has survived from lootings and decay to show that the Shang king, like an Egyptian pharaoh, went into the afterlife accompanied by many precious objects of bronze, jade and stone.

Even at its height, the Shang state probably controlled a relatively small area of northern China, although it was much more widely influential as a model for aspiring rivals. The Shang system appears to have been a form of feudalism, in which royal relatives and other lords held their lands in return for allegiance and service. Greater centralization may have prevailed for a time under the Zhou (Chou) dynasty, which overthrew the Shang in 1027 BC. The Zhou power base lay to the west of the Shang heartland, in the Wei valley. Further west were barbarian peoples, and Zhou's position as a buffer state probably helped to sustain its vigour; in the history of China and many other lands, semi-civilized border states have often taken over and renewed a failing central culture.

Over the next few centuries, following a familiar pattern, Zhou authority gradually declined and the power of local lords grew. In 771 BC rebellious vassals and nomadic raiders attacked the Zhou capital, Hao, killing King You and overrunning the Wei valley. Though greatly weakened, the dynasty survived, transferring its capital to Luoyang in the east; taking their cue from this geographical shift, historians divide the history of the dynasty into the Western Zhou (1027–771 BC) and the Eastern Zhou (771–256 BC) periods.

During the Eastern Zhou period, royal prestige was based not on political power but on reverence for the king's sacred function as 'The Son of Heaven'. The great lordships along the Wei and Yellow River valleys developed into a multitude of states that were effectively independent and almost constantly at war with one another. Chinese historians distinguish between the Spring and Autumn (771–464 BC) and the Warring States (464–222 BC) periods, but these eloquent titles were taken from two Chinese chronicles of events, and the distinction seems to have no special significance in political or military terms.

This was also true of culture and technology, spheres in which the Eastern Zhou witnessed major advances; as so often in human history, an age of bloodshed and misery seemed positively to stimulate creativity. Bronze, lacquer and silk had made their appearance under the Shang; during the Eastern Zhou period, iron tools and weapons were introduced, canals and irrigation systems were constructed, the first money came into use, cities and trade flourished, and technical improvements such as efficient ploughs and horse harnesses made labour more productive. The most influential Chinese thinker, Confucius (c. 552–479 BC), came on the scene, followed in short order by philosophers who disputed his view of duty and piety as the foundation of the

good state, and by the Daoist religion which promoted a more spontaneous, individualistic attitude towards the world. Consequently, by the end of the Eastern Zhou period, important aspects of traditional China had already appeared.

Meanwhile dog-eat-dog warfare reduced the many 'Warring States' to a handful of kingdoms jostling one another all along the Wei and Yellow River valleys. For a time, shifting alliances maintained a balance of power among them which prevented any one state from becoming too strong. But once more the border states were favoured, since they could expand at the expense of their less organized non-Chinese neighbours. By the late 4th century it was clear that either Qin in the far west, or Chu, expanding south from the Yangtze valley, was likely to achieve supremacy and, perhaps, empire.

Below: mottled white jade plaque from the 3rd century BC. From the earliest times the Chinese were fascinated by this hard, intensely tactile material, which is found in a range of colours.

帝 皇 始 秦

The First Emperor is shown as appropriately fierce in this 17th-century imaginary portrait. The Chinese have mixed feelings about Shi Huangdi, a bloodthirsty tyrant but also the creator of the empire.

THE FIRST EMPEROR

In 771 BC the Zhou dynasty had abandoned its western base to invaders from the steppe, and had moved east. Eventually the Zhou territories were recovered by the Qin, or Ch'in, a noble family who used their acquired power-base to create a powerful monarchy. As well as being an expansionist frontier society, Qin became a centralized state of a new type. Its policies were shaped by the principles of Legalism, a philosophy first put into practice by the minister Shang Yang (d. 338 BC). By contrast with the ethical approach of Confucianism, Legalism advocated the strengthening of the state by all means, relying above all on force and terror: concentration of resources, military might, iron discipline and the severest possible punishments. In the case of Qin, Legalist policies also included the breaking of the nobles' power, military promotion on the basis of merit, and a series of great public works designed to boost agricultural productivity.

Such policies are often brilliantly successful in the short or even the medium run, and from the late 4th century BC Qin went from strength to strength. Coalitions of enemy states were beaten back, and in 312 Qin won a crushing victory over the powerful Chu. Other sometime rivals – Han, Wei, Zhao – became client states, and in 256 the Qin army finally snuffed out the weak but previously sacrosanct Zhou dynasty.

In 246 BC the youthful Prince Zheng (259–210 BC) came to the throne of Qin. In 230 his armies began a final ten-year campaign, during which all six of the remaining rival states were defeated and annexed. Master of the entire

Chinese world (though a much smaller world than it would later become), in 221 BC Zheng pronounced himself Shi Huangdi, First Emperor, and decreed that his descendants should hold the title of Huangdi (emperor, literally 'august personage') down the generations.

At his right hand the emperor had an able adviser of the Legalist school, Li Si, who was probably responsible for detailed policy-making. But it seems quite certain that ultimate power rested with Shi Huangdi himself, and that the wide-ranging reforms and totalitarian excesses of his reign were direct expressions of the emperor's tyrannical will.

The creation of a strong, centralized, obedient state was carried through with ruthless logic. A thoroughgoing attempt was made to destroy traditional authority in the conquered kingdoms. Some 120,000 noble families are said to have been imported and resettled in the new imperial capital, Xianyang, under the Emperor's eye. The empire was divided into provinces or 'commanderies' whose boundaries cut across those of the former kingdoms. The new provinces were run by imperial governors, while administration at all levels was entrusted to a hierarchy of officials; thus China's celebrated imperial bureaucracy came into being as an extension of the efficient system developed in Qin. Central control was also furthered by a network of roads which radiated from the capital to the ends of the empire. The laws were codified and applied to all the Emperor's subjects; for many unfortunates, the benefits of uniformity were outweighed by the savagery of the punishments, inflicted for the slightest shortcoming. Uniform weights and measures, and a uniform coinage, were unambiguous advances except in so far as they simplified the task of the tax collector.

The interests of the Qin emperor and his people most nearly coincided in the economic sphere. Road- and canal-building, and irrigation and reclamation schemes, improved communications and led to increased production and better distribution of food and other products. At times, imperial reforms showed a surprisingly imaginative grasp of detail, as in the apparently trivial decree stipulating that all carts were to be made

with the same axle-length. Accepting ruts in roads as a fact of life, the decree ensured that the ruts would be the same distance apart as the wheels of any cart that drove over them; consequently the wheels would either fit into the ruts or miss them altogether, but would not lurch into a single rut and tilt or overturn!

Shi Huangdi's most celebrated feat was the building of the Great Wall of China, still regarded as one of the wonders of the world. The main external threat to China came from nomadic peoples who descended from the northern steppes and forests, and defensive walls had already been raised by some Chinese kingdoms during the Warring States period. Shi Huangdi's labour force in fact linked three substantial existing walls, but it also extended them over vast distances; even if slightly qualified, the emperor's achievement in creating a 4,000-kilometre fortification all along the northern frontier remains a mighty one. Completed in 214 BC, the Wall is also a monument to the emperor's disregard for human suffering, since tens of thousands of forced labourers are known to have died during its construction. Present-day photographs tend to be misleading, since many impressive stretches of the Wall are the result of rebuilding by the Ming

Burning books and burying scholars alive: these infamous acts of the First Emperor were never forgotten or forgiven by the Confucian elite that provided China's governing class. They are shown in this painting on silk as parts of a single scene.

and later regimes. The Qin structure was a more basic affair, made from a material widely used by the Chinese: earth. Loose earth was placed between boards and pounded repeatedly until it became compact and hard. The 'bricks' created by this operation were astonishingly durable, and had been used since Shang times for city walls, platforms on which prestigious buildings were raised, and fortifications.

The Great Wall, and the roads and canals constructed on Shi Huangdi's orders, were incredibly labour-intensive projects. And there were many others, notably the hundreds of palaces and gardens said to have graced the emperor's capital; even the thousands of noble families-in-exile at Xianyang were encouraged to renew their past glories by creating lavish imitations of the palaces they had occupied in their homelands. Forced labour on the scale required by Shi Huangdi was certainly unpopular, but few dared to criticize or oppose the emperor. Thought and speech were as closely monitored as actions, despite the existence of long-established literary and philosophical schools. An infamous 'Burning of the Books' in 213 BC signalled the emperor's intention to destroy the potentially subversive

Opposite: the Great Wall of China, winding endlessly across the mountains north of Beijing. Though originally created in the 3rd century BC by the first emperor, Shi Huangdi, the Great Wall in its present condition, faced with stone and brick, dates from the Ming period (1368–1644).

Above: an atmospheric 19th-century view of the Great Wall of China, in an engraving by the British artist Thomas Allom. Most sections of the 4,000-kilometre-long wall are about 7 or 8 metres high and 7 metres thick.

Confucian tradition and restrict Chinese history to the annals of Qin; the old kingdoms, already dismantled, were to be erased from human memory. Outside the imperial library, the only books available to the emperor's subjects were to be the history of Qin and politically neutral disquisitions on practical subjects such as agriculture and

medicine. The following year, over four hundred Confucian scholars are said to have been buried alive for real or imaginary offences. When the emperor's eldest son, Fu Su, dared to object, he was sent north in disgrace to supervise further work on the Great Wall; and in the event his absence from the centre of power cost him the throne and his life.

Some books did survive, despite bloodcurdling penalties for harbouring them; and so did the Confucian tradition, which became one of the central facts of Chinese life. Confucian portrayals of Shi Huangdi were understandably vitriolic, and for most of Chinese history the emperor was usually reviled as a monster and only occasionally praised as the maker of the Chinese state. Of course Shi Huangdi was both monster and maker, characteristics of strong-minded tyrants that have recurred throughout history.

The emperor's personal habits, shaped by paranoia and superstition, are also reminiscent of more recent dictators. Having survived several attempts to assassinate him, Shi Huangdi became increasingly restless and secretive. He had a multiple-palace complex constructed, linked by covered passages, within which he could move swiftly, his whereabouts uncertain enough to make him safe from assassins and evil spirits. He also travelled within his realm incognito, or even in disguise, sleeping at a different location every night; only Li Si and the chief eunuch, Zhao Gao, were permitted to know where he was, and any temporary host or bystander who revealed his knowledge was instantly put to death.

The emperor's obsessions seem to have become paramount quite soon after he adopted his title. The '-di' element in Shi Huangdi contains a strong suggestion of divinity, and the emperor took the possibility seriously. Confronted with his own mortality, he adopted a dual strategy, desperately seeking the Elixir of Life while simultaneously preparing for himself the grandest tomb that absolute power could command. His craving for immortality made the inaccessible emperor ready to listen to magicians and charlatans, and some recorded incidents suggest that on occasion he fell victim to confidence tricksters. One group of seers told him that there were

enchanted islands in the eastern seas where, thanks to the long-sought Elixir, old age and death were unknown. Shi Huangdi responded by despatching a fleet to find the islands, present their inhabitants with rich gifts, and bring back the miraculous draught; presumably it never occurred to the emperor that, if they met with success, the captain and crew were more likely to take advantage of the Elixir's properties for their own benefit than to preserve it for their master. In time the fleet returned, having allegedly reached the enchanted islands; but the expedition leader explained that the gifts he had brought had not been lavish enough to persuade the immortals to part with their secret. Impressed, the emperor sent out an even greater fleet, loaded down with wealth. It set sail, and was never heard of again.

Shi Huangdi died in 210 BC, at the early age of fifty, while making a characteristically unpublicized inspection of the eastern provinces. Li Si and Zhao Gao kept the news a secret for their own purposes, arranging for the emperor's body to be quietly brought back to the capital by road; the imperial litter was preceded by a cartload of fish to disguise the smell of decomposition. He was buried in the tomb prepared over the years, like so many of his works, by hundreds of thousands of forced labourers. The tomb is now a huge mound of earth, known as Mount Li, but this was originally the centre of a great above-ground 'Spirit City' with pavilions, temples, towers and walls, dedicated to the cult of the emperor. The inside of the tomb, according to later writers, was a microcosm of the world, with representations of the heavens on the ceiling and a landscaped floor with rivers and seas of mercury which flowed under the impulse of some mechanical contrivance. Needless to say, the tomb was crammed with fabulous wealth and wonderfully fashioned objects; and, as in all the best archaeological adventure

Below: the 'Terracotta Army', part of a 6,000-strong force of ceramic warriors discovered in 1974–7. Arranged in military formation in large pits, they guarded the tomb of the First Emperor.

stories, intruders were reported to risk being impaled by bolts from crossbows, set to fire in response to any disturbance of the tomb.

These tall tales acquired a sudden plausibility in 1974, when people digging a well uncovered the 'Terracotta Army' – thousands of life- or over-life-size ceramic warriors, lined up in formation below ground. Two more pits were found in 1976–7 at the same site, about 1,500 metres east of Mount Li, and it is clear that this army of at least 6,000 men had been assembled to serve the First Emperor in the afterlife. Nothing had been skimped. Every face was that of an individual, and it has been suggested that actual soldiers sat for their ceramic portraits. The men – archers, foot-soldiers and cavalry – were equipped with real weapons and accompanied by chariots drawn by splendidly modelled horses four abreast.

The artisans who knew the layout of Shi Huangdi's tomb are said to have been silenced by being buried alive in it. If so, they died in vain, for the tomb was looted in the upheavals that soon followed on the emperor's death; the weapons of the Terracotta Army, being of superior quality and in full working order, proved to be a prime attraction.

The Qin Emperor had expected his dynasty to reign for ten thousand generations. In the event it proved to be more vulnerable and shorter-lived than he can ever have dreamed.

Above: the Terracotta Army in rank after rank, ready to fight spirit enemies of the emperor. Horses with knotted tails originally stood four abreast in the tomb, harnessed to a chariot.

Left: kneeling archer, one of the many striking figures in the Terracotta Army, individually characterized and originally equipped with real weapons.

The Confucian ideal: the emperor as scholar, translating classic texts in the company of his fellow-literati; painting on silk. In later times the Han were regarded as the model dynasty.

THE HAN ERA

The rapid decline of the Qin dynasty was largely the fault of the First Emperor himself. He had intended his eldest son, Fu Su, to succeed him but, living and dying in secrecy, he inadvertently made possible a palace coup. While the emperor's death remained unannounced, the chief minister, Li Si, and the eunuch Zhao Gao acted to secure the throne for their own candidate. Communications purporting to be from the emperor himself were sent to Fu Su and the powerful general Meng Tian, ordering them to commit suicide. They obeyed, and the conspirators

secured the throne for another of Shi Huangdi's twenty sons, who ascended as Ershi Huangdi.

The new emperor has generally been portrayed as effete and incompetent, but it is possible that he was simply a victim of circumstances. In a power struggle at court, Li Si was outmanoeuvred by Zhao Gao; in accordance with the Legalist precepts which the veteran minister had himself promoted, he and his entire family, even to the remotest relations, were cruelly put to death in 208 BC. The following year Zhao Gao forced the second emperor to commit suicide and attempted to usurp the throne, but his lack of any legitimate claim (and probably the fact that he was a eunuch, mutilated in order that he should serve rather than command) prompted a widespread refusal to obey his orders. Zhao Gao bowed to the inevitable and handed over the imperial seal to one of Shi Huangdi's nephews.

The new sovereign enjoyed his position for only a few weeks. Despite the incidental prosperity created by Qin totalitarianism, the regime of forced labour and savage punishments bred resentments that surfaced as soon as the apparently irresistible Shi Huangdi was removed. The first serious rebellion broke out in 209 BC, reputedly led by conscripts who realized that they would be late in reporting for duty; certain that they would suffer for it, they took up arms with the determination of men who had nothing to lose. Large areas of China were soon disaffected, and some of the kingdoms destroyed by Shi Huangdi reappeared and began to re-establish themselves as independent powers.

One of these kingdoms, Han, was ruled by Liu Bang, an illiterate villager who had climbed to power as the Qin empire decayed. In 206 BC Liu Bang's troops captured Xiangyang, and shortly afterwards the imperial family was massacred, Shi Huangdi's tomb was looted, and the capital was burned to the ground; the destruction of the imperial library meant that the only copies of many banned books were lost forever or only returned to circulation in uncertain reconstructions. Having seized the nerve-centre of the empire, Liu Bang eliminated his rivals and in 202 BC proclaimed himself first emperor of the Han dynasty; he became known to history by his posthumous name, Gaozu.

Although Gaozu and his associates had risen from the lower orders, the new dynasty maintained the existing social fabric and governed through a modified version of Qin institutions. From this time onwards the Confucian conception of benign, responsible rule prevailed in theory, but Legalist exaltation of the state and ruthless realism inevitably re-emerged when vital interests were at stake. Confucian ideas permeated the official class, which assumed its classic form as an elite of scholar-bureaucrats; a further

touch would be added later in the dynasty (165 BC), when the first imperial examinations were held, confirming the link between scholarship and office which became the most distinctive feature of imperial Chinese government.

The first Han emperor hardly seemed likely to favour scholars; when presented with distinguished Confucians he had been known to collect their hats and ostentatiously urinate into them. His change of attitude was probably gradual, but has been encapsulated in a single episode. When his chamberlain repeatedly quoted from the classics, Gaozu said with martial irritability, 'I conquered the empire on horseback, and scorned the wisdom contained in old books.' The chamberlain, Lu Jia, replied, 'That is true; but your Majesty will not be able to govern it on horseback,' and pointed out that the Qin had fallen because they had not ruled with wisdom or

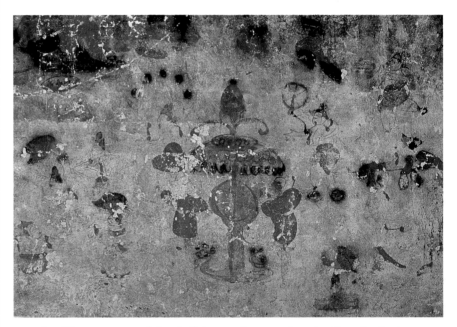

restraint. The emperor took heed of the warning and began to place greater reliance on the talents of the intelligentsia.

The Han came to be seen as the model dynasty, presiding over a wealthy, peaceful, far-flung empire. But its future seemed less certain during its early decades. Having seized power, Gaozu could not avoid handing out large fiefs to his relatives and supporters; this partly re-created the feudal system of the Zhou era, which was only slowly dismantled by subsequent Han emperors. A more serious weakness was the dynastic instability

Everyday life under the Han: a scene from a tomb painting. Much of our information about the period comes from objects intended for the afterlife.

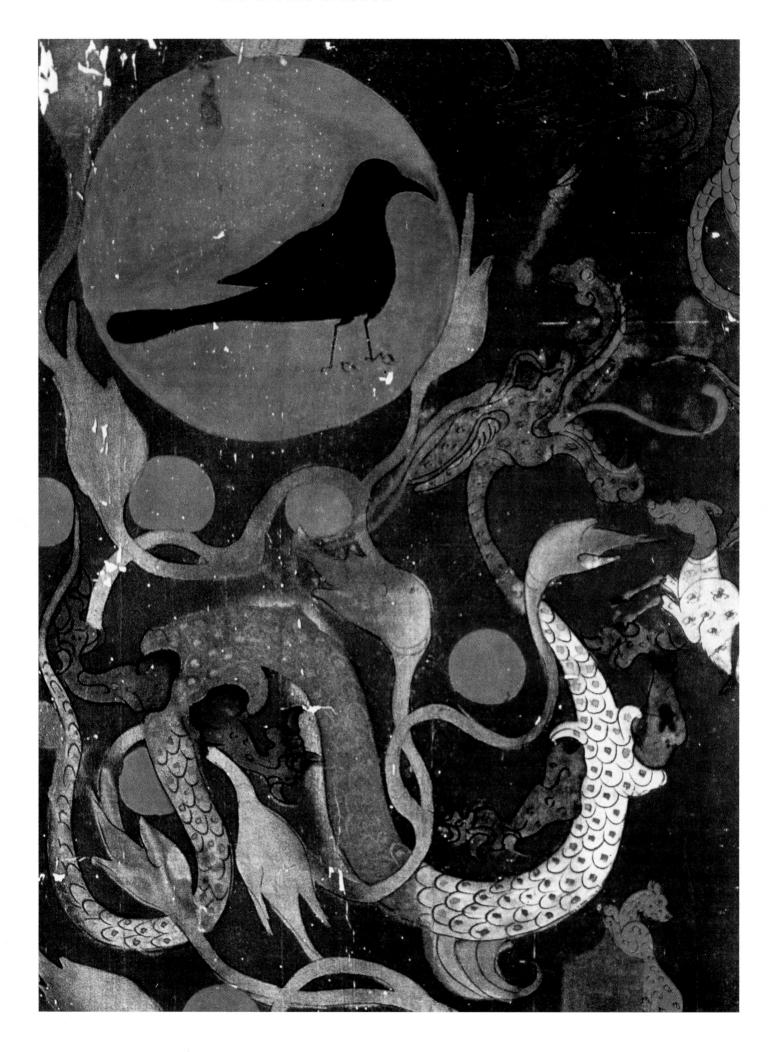

that was always latent in a situation where emperors fathered many sons by a variety of women. During Gaozu's last years, a behind-the-scenes struggle took place between Lu, who had borne the emperor's eldest son, and the rising favourite Qi, who hoped to win the succession for her own child. Although the emperor's amatory preference was clear, Lu was a more able intriguer than her rival; it was even said that when the succession was being debated, the learned men recruited by Lu to plead her cause were supplied with whispered arguments by the empress herself – from behind a screen, since it would have been unthinkable for a woman to take any public role in decision-making.

When Gaozu died in 195 BC, the succession remained with Lu's son. Now Empress Dowager, she was able to take a cruel revenge on her rival and effectively rule China. When her son died, she installed a boy emperor, and when he grew old enough to become a nuisance, she had him despatched and replaced by another child. Meanwhile she tried to put her relatives in an unchallengeable position, removing noble families in bloody purges and giving their estates to her own kin. By contrast, the severities of the Qin legal code were progressively reduced, perhaps in a bid to make the new status quo popular among the masses. Lu remained in power until her death in 180 BC, but her posthumous plans went disastrously wrong. In the desperate struggle that ensued, the losers were the Empress Dowager's family, all of whom suffered the usual fate of complete annihilation.

With the accession of Wendi (180–157 BC), the Han dynasty resumed control. Wendi was remembered as one of the 'virtuous emperors', and under his successor, Jingdi (157–141) and above all the long-lived Wudi (141–87), the Han era reached its apogee. A feudal uprising, the Rebellion of the Seven Kingdoms (154), was

crushed and the fiefs brought under control; in 127 a new decree laid down that all male children of such magnates were to share the inheritance equally, a shrewd measure which quickly reduced the size of lordships. Steady Chinese colonization of the South accelerated the process of sinification, making this vast, rice-rich area an integral part of the empire, culturally as well as politically. The armies of Wudi, 'the Martial Emperor', pushed even further, into Vietnam and Korea,

Left: the world of myth (The Legend of the Nine Sons), pictured on a silk hanging found in a Han tomb. After two millennia, it is in astonishingly good condition.

Watch and ward. This green-glazed pottery model of a tower, found in a Han dynasty tomb, was made in three detachable sections. As in ancient Egypt, the dead in Han China were buried with everything they might need in the afterlife.

Left: a unique funeral suit, one of a pair worn by the Han prince Liu Sheng and his wife. Each was made from 2,000 pieces of jade, held together by gold thread.

Below: remains of a beacon tower on the Silk Road at Dunhuang. Travellers from China were safe until they left this western outpost of the empire and set out across Central Asia.

and also took the offensive against the barbarians beyond the Great Wall. There the Xiongnu, a powerful confederation of nomad tribes, had become so dangerous by the early Han period that Gaozu had adopted a policy of appeasement, sending gifts to the barbarians and even giving their leader a Chinese princess in marriage. (To Chinese sensibilities this was the equivalent to a living death, so much so that the lament of a bride given to foreigners became one of the staples of

their poetry.) When Wudi decided to confront the Xiongnu, his armies won striking victories, but it was far from clear that the threat from the elusive nomads had been eliminated. The fact was tacitly acknowledged when the Great Wall was extended and refurbished by the addition of signal towers. The extended wall ran far to the west, shielding from the barbarians a long, narrow strip of recently-won Chinese territory that skirted Tibet. Along this travelled Chinese caravans carrying silks and other goods on the first stage of a journey to Central Asia and beyond; this was the famous Silk Road, which would soon indirectly link Han China with the Roman Empire, on the other side of the known world. Chinese merchants never travelled the full distance, but some did get as far as Persia. The Chinese view of the world was also broadened by the reports brought back from Afghanistan by the ambassador-explorer Zhang Qian, which described an exotic land of elephants – India – and suggested that it might be reached from South China.

For all its splendour, the long reign of Wudi showed the first signs that the dynasty had passed its zenith. Wendi and Jingdi had heeded their ministers' advice that it was unwise to place over-heavy burdens on the peasantry (although archae-ological excavations in the early 1990s revealed that Han imperial burials were tremendous undertakings, albeit not quite on the scale of Shi Huangdi's). But Wudi's military expeditions, large-scale population transfers and embellish-ment of the Han capital, Changan, evidently strained the imperial budget. In 117 BC the iron and salt industries were turned into profitable state monopolies, and Wudi later initiated a number of money-raising schemes that were a good deal less reputable.

As so often, the strong ruler held on to power until his death, and it was his descendants who paid for his excesses. Military reverses and palace intrigues complicated Wudi's last years, and in subsequent reigns the state was undermined by familiar harem rivalries and blood purges. In AD 9 one member of a former empress's family, Wang Mang, was able to seize power and found a new dynasty, the Xin. His timing proved unfor-tunate, since he soon faced peasant insurrections, intensified by resentment at the expansion of a new landowning class at the expense of small farmers, and by the devastating effects of floods followed by prolonged drought. Natural catastro-phes tended to be seen as Heaven's verdict on a dynasty or a usurper (that is, a failed dynast). Wang Mang decreed far-ranging reforms intended to curb the landowners, including the imperial ownership of all land, justifying this 'nationalization' and other measures by invoking

the supposed practices of the Zhou era. His poli-cies only alienated the wealthy landowners, swelling the coalition ranged against him. Finally, in AD 23 a rebel peasant army, the Red Eyebrows, captured Changan and put Wang Mang to death.

The Han dynasty was resurrected by Guangwu Di (25–58), who suppressed the Red Eyebrows and, after eleven years of campaigning, brought all the breakaway and dissident areas back under imperial control. Since the history of the dynasty falls into two distinct parts, the earlier is known as the Former or Western Han (202 BC–9 AD) and the restored dynasty as the Later or Eastern Han (AD 25–220). The geographical terms reflect the transfer of the capital from Changan in the Wei valley to Luoyang. The continuities of early Chinese history are illustrated by the fact that a similar shift had occurred over seven hun-dred years earlier, under the Zhou; and in fact the sites of the two dynasties' later capitals were nearly identical.

The Han restoration brought peace and stabil-ity for most of the 1st century. A vigorous imper-ial government worked with the rising landed class while foreign trade flourished and new influ-ences, including Buddhism, entered China. Then the endemic imperial disorder – weak or child-sovereigns, surrounded by ambitious consorts and courtiers – appeared again. Wealthy landowners and Confucian officials also attempted to win influence, but nearness to the imperial person gave consorts or palace eunuchs a powerful, if pre-carious, advantage. For a time the eunuchs were paramount, but in 189 a coup led to a wholesale massacre that broke their power.

Meanwhile a new rural crisis had already begun and, coming at a time of imperial weak-ness, would again bring down the dynasty. Hundreds of thousands of peasants rallied to a messianic Daoist sect, the Yellow Turbans, which staged a rebellion in 184. A group of imperial generals, already the strong men of the founder-ing regime, took the field and fought one another as well as the Yellow Turbans. Han emperors sur-vived as puppets until 220, when the last of the line was deposed and the generals began to divide up China among themselves.

Beauty of form. All the details have been obliterated from this carved wooden figure, made during the Former Han period; but it remains a thing of numinous loveliness.

The Sui emperor Yangdi sailing on the Grand Canal, which was essentially his creation; 18th-century painting on silk. The Canal was certainly the most enduring achievement of the short-lived Sui dynasty.

SUI & TANG

The Han dynasty had reigned for over four hundred years, interrupted only once by the brief usurpation of Wang Mang. The era had witnessed long periods of prosperity, and had been notable for advances in iron manufacture, hydraulics, papermaking and international trade. Its influence was still greater than this suggests since, ever afterwards, the Chinese regarded a unified empire as the norm, even when periods of disunity lasted for hundreds of years. Henceforth they would call themselves 'Sons of Han', and in many respects they regarded the Han empire as the model for future ages, much as people in the West tended to measure everything by the standards of ancient Greece and Rome. The fall of the Han, like the fall of the Roman Empire, was followed by a long

The Grand Canal, a thousand years after the Sui period and still a vital artery of Chinese communications. This engraving shows the late 18th-century British embassy passing through a sluice on its way to Beijing.

period of obscure struggles that might be described as Dark Ages. Peasant uprisings and civil wars disrupted trade and manufactures and undermined the urban economies; Luoyang itself, the capital, went up in flames. The states that replaced the empire were less centralized but nevertheless eager to take on rivals, so that the 360-year period down to AD 581 featured struggles between landowners and peasants, military men and the large numbers of non-ethnic Chinese who had been settled in the North, officials and local rulers. Regimes came and went in a bewildering fashion, as even the following, much-simplified outline demonstrates. After the disappearance of the Han, China was divided into three kingdoms: Wei in the North, Shu in the southwest, and Wu in the South. The Chinese have long been fascinated by the personalities, conflicts and feats of arms of this period, embodied in a famous 14th-century novel, *The Romance of the Three Kingdoms*; actual historical figures move through its pages, plotting and fighting for survival as they play out their roles as the cruel militarist, the all-wise royal adviser and the death-defying hero.

The period ended when Wei conquered first Shu (263) and later Wu (280), briefly reuniting China under the Western Jin dynasty (280–316). In 316 fragmentation began again when a partly sinicized steppe people overran the North, which was then subject to a succession of regimes; the period 304–439, for example, carries the daunting label 'The Sixteen Kingdoms of the Five Barbarians'. In the South, the former imperial dynasty continued until 420 as the Eastern Jin, after which the political situation was almost as volatile as in the North, where the Northern Wei were replaced by the Zhou and the Ji, whose conflict ended in victory for the Northern Zhou.

Finally, in 581, an ambitious general overthrew the Northern Zhou. He went on to conquer the South in 589, re-uniting China and becoming, as Wendi, the first emperor of the Sui dynasty. This ended a four-hundred-year period of disunity that has sometimes been dismissed as a merely chaotic interval between great dynasties. It was certainly an age of rising and falling states and sometimes appalling bloodshed (perhaps not very different in either respect from the last four hundred years of European history). But it also witnessed an efflorescence of Chinese literature and art, and some radical cultural changes. The most significant development of all was the establishment and naturalization of Buddhism; despite occasional turmoils, this Indian religion became an integral part of the Chinese way of life, in which Confucian, Daoist and Buddhist values complemented rather than struggled to overcome

Above: This crowded, intricately carved stone comes from a 7th-century Chinese burial, but the style is Persian or Near Eastern – a striking example of the cosmopolitan Tang outlook.

Opposite: the stone doorway of a Tang period tomb, with superbly carved real and mythical creatures. The symmetrical dragon above the lintel was a highly stylized, centuries-old motif.

one another. Some of the greatest masterpieces of Chinese Buddhist art – cave-temples, murals, sculptures and scrolls – began to be produced during the period of disunity in the famous Thousand-Buddha Caves of Dunhuang, at the Chinese end of the Silk Road.

The relatively brief reign of the first Sui emperor transformed China's political fortunes. Wendi (589–604) had all the furious ruthlessness that the age demanded. On the death of his son-in-law, the Northern Zhou emperor, he wiped out all fifty-nine of his imperial relatives and seized the throne for himself. He built a new capital at Changan, on almost the same site as its Han predecessor. Having conquered the South, he centralized the administration and attempted to make it more efficient and merit-based; since he was capable of personally beating to death any official who displeased him, Wendi's reforms had a marked effect, at least in the short run. Above all, while successfully keeping China's enemies at bay, he promoted shrewd policies aimed at minimizing the differences that had grown up between Northern and Southern traditions.

Despite his violent character, Wendi figures in Chinese histories as one of the good emperors, since he united and strengthened the country and died in possession of the throne. His son and successor, Yangdi (605–17), had the opposite reputation, one that is arguably based on his final failure rather than any great difference between his abilities and policies and those of his father. Yangdi intrigued his way to the throne, gaining

the succession at the expense of his elder brother and possibly doing away with Wendi before the old emperor had a chance to change his mind. Yangdi pursued most of Wendi's policies, if anything more vigorously – possibly too vigorously and impetuously. Apeing his father, he built a secondary capital at Luoyang. Wendi had made repairs to the Great Wall and had built some canals, but Yangdi surpassed him in both areas. Large-scale work on the Wall is said to have employed a million men and cost thousands of lives; and the building of the Grand Canal, linking the Yellow and Yangtze Rivers, was a major feat which ensured that the emperor and the great cities of the North could be kept supplied with the bounty of the lower Yangtze and the South, which were beginning to rival the North in agricultural productivity.

These and other grand projects went hand in hand with an aggressive foreign policy that brought spectacular results – and then met with disaster. In 612–14 a series of land and sea campaigns against the kingdom of Koguryo, straddling Manchuria and Korea, ended in costly failures; and these encouraged new activity on the part of the hitherto submissive people living beyond the Great Wall. At this period the restless barbarians were the Eastern Turks, who in 615 besieged and almost captured the emperor himself. By this time the peasant revolts that so often signalled the end of a dynasty had broken out over much of North China. Yangdi sailed south and held out at Yangzhou until he was assassinated in 619. Since his short-lived successor was only a puppet of the dynasty-to-be, the brief glory of the Sui was already over.

Yangdi evidently over-extended Chinese resources, and his exploitation of forced labour seems to have been as callous as that of Shi Huangdi some eight hundred years before. But the portrayal of Yangdi as a 'bad' emperor mainly stems from Chinese political theory, which could only justify a change of dynasty by labelling the last emperor of a line as a degenerate who had deservedly forfeited 'the Mandate of Heaven'. Consequently the last Sui emperor was by definition worthless, just as the first emperor of the succeeding Tang dynasty could only be supremely

武則天

Less sweet than she looks: the Empress Wu was the only woman to rule China as the sovereign in her own right. She manipulated and set aside her own sons and destroyed most of the Tang royal family; yet she survived her own deposition and died of old age.

worthy. A less high-minded interpretation of the relationship between the dynasties is possible. Since the Tang took over the Sui infrastructure and institutions, they benefited from Sui achievements – above all from the existence of the Grand Canal – without incurring the blame for the blood and suffering which had made them possible. So it can be argued that the ruthlessness of the one regime laid the groundwork for the splendour and stability of the next. Since the relationship between the earlier Qin and Han dynasties was not dissimilar, this is perhaps a historical phenomenon that warrants further investigation.

The founder of the Tang dynasty was a general, Li Yuan, in charge of the northern border defences. When Yangdi fled south, Li Yuan marched on Changan, where he first installed a puppet Sui emperor (617–18) and then assumed the title himself. As Gaozu (618–26), he spent much of his reign overcoming rivals and restoring the Sui administrative system. He owed a good deal to the military abilities of his sons, notably Li Shimin, who is traditionally credited with advising his father that he must seize the throne at the propitious moment: 'Fulfil the desire of the people, raise a righteous army, and transform calamity into glory!'

Righteousness was less in evidence during the dynastic in-fighting of the mid-620s, which culminated in the elimination of Li Shimin's brothers and the enforced abdication of Gaozu. Li Shimin became the Emperor Taizong (626–49), and proved an able, energetic ruler. He laid the groundwork for the political and cultural achievements that made the Tang period one of China's great ages. Prosperity at home and expansion abroad continued under Taizong's successor, Gaozong (649–83), thanks to the sound administrative structure. Able ministers and officials must have been responsible for one of the greatest Tang achievements, the legal code first issued in 653, which influenced all later law-making in China as well as in most of East Asia. The emperor is unlikely to have contributed much to the work, since he is known to have been ailing and increas-

ingly under the influence of his remarkable empress, Wu.

Wu is said to have begun her career in the harem of her husband's father, Taizong. On the death of Gaozong she continued to rule through her sons, Zhongzong and Ruizong; each was deposed in turn, and in 690, having wiped out most of the Tang royal family, she cast aside all pretence and had herself openly proclaimed as China's ruler. Although Chinese history records

Left: Buddhist art. Under the Tang dynasty, Buddhism became a major influence on Chinese life. Masterpieces of painting such as this 10th-century royal portrait are preserved at Dunhuang.

Below: a Buddhist caravan being attacked by robbers; a detail from a Tang dynasty wall painting at Dunhuang. This was a far-western outpost of Tang China where Buddhist cave temples were cut into the cliffs from the 4th century AD onwards.

Glazed pottery camel from a Tang dynasty tomb. Superbly observed and characterized animals are a feature of Tang art. The camel became a familiar sight in the trade-conscious north-west.

officials who owed everything to the existing regime. By the early 700s Wu was in her seventies and becoming increasingly arbitrary and swayed by favourites. Finally, in 705, she was deposed in a palace coup and the former puppet-emperor Zhongzong was restored to the throne. Neither he nor his successor, Ruizong, seem to have got over their early domination by Wu, and their reigns were shot through with intrigues and corrupt dealings worthy of an Italian Renaissance court, in which poisonings and suicides marked the rise and fall of emperors, their designing relatives, and ministers and favourites.

The ultimate winner in these vicious power-games became known to history as 'the Mysterious Ancestor', Xuanzong (712–56). A son of Ruizong, he was yet another Chinese sovereign who followed a bloodthirsty debut with a record of intelligent and benevolent rule. A series of reforms restored the administration and the imperial finances, the Tang legal code was cast into its definitive form and, with the emperor himself setting the example, cultural and religious enthusiasms flourished as never before.

In fact, Xuanzong's reign proved to be the climax of the Tang golden age. For almost 150 years China was simultaneously the greatest power in Asia and the centre of a splendid cosmopolitan culture that was something new in the country's history. Chinese armies thrust into Central Asia, further westward than they had ever marched. Their fortunes fluctuated, but generally speaking Turks, Khitans and Tibetans were kept at bay and the kingdoms of East and South-East Asia acknowledged Tang suzerainty and mimicked Tang culture. Great powers such as Byzantium and Sassanid Persia maintained diplomatic relations with China. Caravans plied up and down the Silk Road through Central Asia, bringing people and ideas as well as goods. Changan became the greatest capital in the world, with a population that may have reached two million. The foreigners who thronged its streets included traders, diplomats, monks, craftsmen, and also refugees from trouble-spots such as the Middle East, where Arabs carrying the new message of Islam were wiping long-established states off the map. Consequently China, for long periods hardly

the activities of many powerful women, Wu was the only female to occupy the throne and rule in her own name.

During the five decades of Wu's predominance, purges and faction-fights caused some disruption, but in the long run the administration was improved by her promotion of officials who had risen through the examination system, in preference to the noble and wealthy classes that still normally held many offices; this was not necessarily an altruistic decision on Wu's part, since the aristocracy of the north-west in particular had strong connections with the Tang and was therefore suspect in its loyalties, unlike the scholar-

aware of the outside world, welcomed Persians and Jews, Arabs and Nestorian Christians, Indian monks and emissaries and mercenaries of many tribal groups.

Perhaps the most powerful cultural impact from outside was made by Buddhism. Despite the fact that it had been known in China for several centuries, it was during this period that it became widespread, and for a time it seemed about to become the dominant Chinese faith. India, the fountainhead of Buddhism, was still remote, and a pilgrim-scholar who reached it became a popular hero and passed into folklore and fiction. This was Xuanzang, or Tripitaka, a monk who took the route across Central Asia and through the north-western passes into India, from which he brought back Buddhist texts that had previously been known by the Chinese only in imperfect versions. However, the most important developments in Chinese Buddhism, such as the great popularity of the salvationist Pure Land doctrine, already owed much to native rather than Indian elements. Buddhism had a turbulent history under the Tang, experiencing extremes of favour and persecution.

The exuberant Tang age produced more than its share of great art, though many of its finest creations – ceramic figures of everyday types, performers, foreigners, animals and fierce guardian spirits – were intended to be seen only by the denizens of the tombs in which they were left to serve. The emperors were themselves patrons of

The Diamond Sutra, a 9th-century Buddhist work, is the oldest known printed text, although the Chinese appear to have produced printed books as early as the 3rd or 4th century AD.

A Tang romance. The picture below is part of a scroll painting in which the Emperor Xuanzong watches his beloved, Yang Guifei, mounting a horse. Regarded by the Chinese as a great love-tragedy, this imperial affair cost Xuanzong his throne and Yang Guifei her life.

the arts, and sometimes executants of the most refined, especially calligraphy. But the greatest artistic creation of the Tang era was its lyric poetry, with its keen appreciation of nature (largely absent from western literature for another thousand years), humour, melancholy, and snap-shot-style of observation, at its finest in the works of Li Bo (701–62) and Du Fu (712–70).

It was the Emperor Xuanzong's misfortune to outlive his own glory. In his later years he fell deeply in love with Yang Guifei, who had formerly been the wife of one of his own sons. An unfortunate consequence was that one of Yang Guifei's cousins, Yang Guozhong, became a rising star at court, although some sort of political equilibrium was maintained for a time, since he was unable to unseat the veteran chief minister, Li Linfu. After Li Linfu's death in 752, Yang Guozhong became chief minister and, coincidentally or otherwise, things began to fall apart. Traditional Chinese histories condemn the Yangs for the catastrophe that ensued, but they were probably less to blame than an inherent weakness in the Tang system, which relied for its security on large armies stationed on the frontiers. To reduce the likelihood of an ambitious general attempting to seize power, command was usually entrusted to semi-barbarian military men with no network of relations and supporters within China. The correctness of the theory came to seem dubious in 755, when An Lushan, a general of mixed Sogdian and Turkish ancestry, came out in revolt; previously ostentatious in his loyalty and greatly favoured by the imperial family, An Lushan may have believed himself threatened by the rapidly increasing power of Yang Guozhong. At the head of the powerful north-eastern army, An Lushan captured Changan in 756. The emperor fled with his court, but his troops compelled him to execute not only Yang Guozhong but his beloved Yang Guifeng. She was allowed to stage-manage her own demise (she was strangled in front of a Buddhist shrine), a stylistic touch which helped to lodge the imperial love-tragedy in the folk memory and make the episode one of the great set-pieces of later Chinese literature.

By sacrificing his favourites Xuanzong retained the loyalty of his troops and saved the dynasty. He abdicated in favour of his son, Suzong (756–62), under whom the internal situation slowly improved. The rebellion became less directly menacing after An Lushan was murdered by his own son, but fighting went on for years and some of the most fertile areas of North China were devastated by the rival armies. The Tang position in Central Asia had been badly weakened when an Arab army overcame the Chinese at the battle of Talas in 751, before the general collapse, and neglect of the far-western territories during the internal power struggles led to large, irreversible losses in the region. Two side-effects of the upheavals were a decline in the long-distance trade across Central Asia and renewed Chinese migration to the South; Canton, already a great southern city, became an entrepôt for the seaborne trade that partly replaced the traffic on the Silk Road.

The Tang dynasty survived the crises of the 750s, but it had passed its zenith. The emperors were forced to accept a situation in which a number of provinces became independent in all but name; as important as the loss of prestige was the loss of tax revenues. The emperors restored some of their authority by creating palace armies to counterbalance the forces on the frontiers; commands were given to eunuch generals, and eunuchs again gradually took control of the imperial government.

Many of the later Tang sovereigns were very young, doubtless reflecting the eunuchs' preference for biddable masters. But even able emperors found it impossible to reform a system that was dominated by vested interests at every level. During the 9th century, the natural disasters that signalled the decay of each Chinese dynasty began to multiply. After a prolonged drought, a popular rebellion broke out in 875. It found a leader in Huang Chao, who ravaged Canton and in 880 captured both Changan and Luoyang in the course of a bloody, spectacular career.

Huang Chao's glory was soon extinguished, but the Tang era was effectively finished, as was

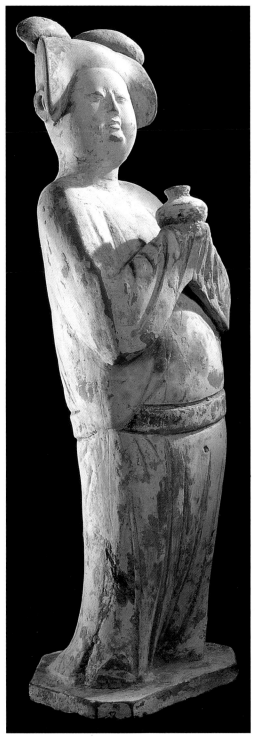

A Tang court lady. Ample proportions such as hers are said to have become fashionable after the plump Yang Guifei became the mistress of the emperor Xuanzong. This was unusual, since slenderness and daintiness were the Chinese ideals of femininity for most of their history.

its fabled capital, Changan. Provincial governors – in effect military strongmen – were now the main contestants for power. One of them, Zhu Wen, a former lieutenant of Huang Chao, seized control of the emperor and massacred the eunuchs. For a time he was content to rule indirectly, but in 907 he assumed the imperial title, disposing of the last shadowy representative of the once-illustrious Tang.

THE SONG

Having installed himself as emperor, the former strongman Zhu Wen enjoyed only five years of power before he was murdered by one of his sons. By 923 his dynasty, the Liang, was extinct. Its authority extended only over North China; in the central and southern regions, rival commanders were busy setting up their own regimes. The political fragmentation of China dated back at least to 880, but until 907 there was a notional unity under the last, helpless Tang emperors. After 907 the fiction of a united empire is abandoned in traditional Chinese histories, which label the half-century down to 960 'The Five Dynasties and Ten Kingdoms'.

As this rather daunting title suggests, the period was one of extreme political vicissitudes. The Five Dynasties ruled in sequence in North China, beginning with Zhu Wen and the Liang.

Each dynasty was founded by a military man, attempted to stabilize the administration and control the army, and fell after two or three reigns when the throne was seized by another officer who founded an equally short-lived dynasty. As so often in the history of civilizations, dynastic ambitions compromised the defences erected against outsiders: in order to make himself emperor, the founder of the third (Jin) dynasty called in a Manchurian people, the Khitans, trading a large area south of the Great Wall for their support. The damage was serious and long term, causing China to endure centuries of insecurity along its northern frontiers.

Of the Ten Kingdoms, nine lay to the south. Their history was only a little less turbulent than that of the Five Dynasties in the North, but some of them were notably successful in generating wealth and managed to keep alive the traditions of Chinese culture.

Nevertheless it was the largest entity, the North, that always seemed most likely to re-unite China. Any one of the later dynasties might have succeeded with a little more luck. The founder of the fourth dynasty, the Han, created a formidable army but died after only three years on the throne. It was usurped by a general, Guo Wei, but the Han managed to survive for a few years with Khitan support in territories close to the northern frontier; this was the tenth of the Ten Kingdoms. Guo Wei (951–54) called his dynasty by the prestigious ancient name of Zhou and clearly intended it to be long-lasting. To prevent future coups he created a corps of elite troops, stationed in the palace and directly under the sovereign's orders. He was succeeded by his adopted son, Chai Rong (954–9), who governed efficiently and began to create a navy. Unluckily for the Zhou, Chai Rong died young, leaving behind an infant who could hardly take direct command of the palace guard. The troops turned to their commander, Zhao Kuangyin, who overcame his feigned or real reluctance and founded the sixth dynasty to have reigned since 907, the Song.

Once again a new imperial house benefited from the efforts of its predecessor and left a far more glorious name to history. Posthumously known as Taizu (960–76), the first Song emperor took over a revitalized state from the Zhou; but it is also true that he acted with energy and skill to make his inheritance permanent, or at any rate as permanent as it is in the nature of dynasties to be. Taizu and his brother and successor, Taizong (976–97), established the dynasty so firmly that, under the Song, child-emperors survived to reign as adults, and familial blood-letting, military coups and eunuch and consort intrigues became relatively infrequent.

Events under the Five Dynasties, including those that had raised Taizu himself to the throne, made it clear that control of the army was essential. The emperor first dealt with the generals whose regional commands made them potentially dangerous, persuading them to take early retirement on generous pensions; the only other option would have been an immediate, unprepared rebellion, launched before the regime had had time to become unpopular. Following the precedent set by the Zhou, Taizu concentrated the best units around the capital, Kaifeng, under his direct command. This made military risings in

Opposite: a beautiful simplicity of form and decoration, the hallmarks of Song ceramics. This Northern Celadon bowl, decorated with a lotus petal relief, is a Northern Song type of stoneware.

Below: bottle and bulb bowl, examples of a ware (Jun) regarded as quite workaday. Its formal perfection and subtly harmonious decoration exemplify the exquisite taste of the Song.

Willows and a distant mountain: painting on silk by Ma Yuan, a great Southern Song master. He was one of the creators of a classic style characterized by fluid brushwork and poetic mist effects.

the provinces much less likely, but it did mean that the Chinese frontiers were manned by inferior troops and were liable to be overrun unless the emperor was on hand with his elite forces. As the northern defences had already been compromised through the territorial concessions made a few years earlier by the Jin, this was potentially a very serious weakness. But fortunately for the Song, the large northern state of Liao, created by China's old enemies the Khitan, refrained from making any aggressive moves during the early decades of the dynasty.

The emperors also patiently eliminated military influence from the administration, waiting until office-holders died or retired and then replacing them with civilian officials. It was during the Song period that the official class acquired the elite characteristics for which it later became celebrated in the outside world. Examinations had been held for centuries, enabling the gifted to rise within the imperial civil service; but the great majority of posts had always been occupied by members of the upper class or their nominees. Under the Song, the examinations were open to more candidates and led on to many more desirable positions in a service which had been reorganized so that it had a rational career structure with prospects of regular promotion. The prizes and prestige involved led to intense competition, and the examinations became major events in the calendar, rigorously conducted so as to prevent cheating or favouritism. Close study of the Confucian classics (the set texts of the examinations) created a class of scholar-officials or literati with a common culture and a refined, artistic cast of mind. Moreover this literati culture became the general possession of the dominant class which had replaced the old aristocracy, absorbing even those members of it who did not take the examinations (or failed them) and did not join the civil service; the situation is roughly comparable with that of the caste of 19th-century Britons, drilled in Greek and Latin, who left school and university to become civil servants, Indian Army officers, colonial officials, and so on. In its own distinctive fashion, Song China acquired a uniquely civilized and civilian ruling class, variously described by historians as gentry, scholar-officials or literati,

and popularly known in the West as mandarins.

The values of the literati soon permeated Chinese society, and its distrust of the military led to a general attitude of disdain for soldiering. Fortunately the first two Song emperors remained martial enough to reunite the country by force of arms. It was done cautiously and gradually, so that the kingdoms to the south were never alarmed enough to coalesce against the Song. The large Southern Tang state was only conquered in 975, shortly before Taizu's death, leaving two relatively small kingdoms that fell to his successor without serious resistance in 978–9. The most important Chinese territory beyond the Song frontiers was the large area within the Great Wall, lost to the Khitan state of Liao during the Five Dynasties period. Taizu made no attempt to dislodge the Khitan, and his successor seems to have gone to war with them reluctantly; although the Song armies made some use of a secret weapon – gunpowder – the Khitan came off better, and when peace was made in 1004 the Chinese agreed to pay them an annual tribute in silver and silk.

The Song never seemed likely to recover the lost territories, let alone repeat the expansive policies of the Han and the Tang. The dynasty's essentially peaceful posture, like its stable government

Naive painting in an age of sophistication. Buddhist art continued to be produced during the Song period in the temple caves at Dunhuang in the far north-west. The charming, busy scenes and strong patterns of the picture above form the strongest possible contrast to Ma Yuan's subtle style, opposite.

and its scholar-officials, made Song China very different from its predecessors. The Song system promoted extraordinary social, economic and cultural advances; or (another way of looking at the same situation) the absence of arbitrary government and great upheavals left the Chinese free to be productive and creative.

The age was one of supreme artistic achievement, for example in the creation of intensely evocative landscape paintings and exquisite porcelain wares. But the material changes were at least as impressive. The population soared to about 100 million. The capital, Kaifeng, became a great commercial as well as imperial-bureaucratic centre; situated east of Luoyang, it stood beside the Grand Canal, where it could be easily supplied with the produce of the increasingly fertile South. In the capital and other cities, trade prospered, and the status of merchants – traditionally regarded as parasites – improved. Industries such as coal mining and shipbuilding operated on a surprisingly large scale. Gunpowder and the magnetic compass were among the useful inventions developed during the period, and printing, discovered somewhat earlier, came into its own; combined with another Chinese invention, paper, it made possible the

wide circulation of the scholarly and literary works which were also characteristic productions of the Song era.

It is worth recalling that all this activity was taking place at a time when Europe was intellectually and technologically backward. If the difference is expressed in competitive terms, China was some five centuries ahead of Europe. Historians have long discussed – without coming to any widely accepted conclusion – why, powered by so many advances, the Chinese economy did not move steadily forward (as Europe's economy was eventually to do) and bring about an industrial revolution in the Far East. Had this happened, of course, the entire history of the world would have been different.

The relative tranquillity of political life under the Song owed much to the first two emperors, who appear to have taken a conscious decision in favour of a civilian power in which the scholar-gentry would play an enhanced role. Future sovereigns were raised in an atmosphere steeped in Confucian values, so that they were less likely to be unhinged by the possession of absolute power; in practice, respect for the experience of their counsellors, and acceptance of the counsellors' duty to voice honest criticism, made the emperor reluctant to behave in fashion seen as arbitrary. As a result, the dynasty enjoyed a continuity in government that had previously been rare, and it survived not only the accession of child-emperors, but the effects of a strain of mental instability in the ruling family.

This political continuity remained the rule even when the general situation became more difficult and disputes over policy led to the creation of factions within the literati. Among the problems that accumulated were the effects of rapid population growth, the increasing power of large landowners and the rising cost of government. Paradoxically, the unmilitary Song maintained an enormous army which ate up most of its revenues, partly in the hope that numbers would compensate for inefficiency and partly, it appears, as a welfare measure, giving employment to hundreds of thousands of the poorest Chinese who might otherwise have become a threat to the security of the regime. The military weakness of the Song

Opposite: the splendour and refinement of the Song. During a festival, the emperor drinks from a cup that has been carved from a precious stone; 17th-century painting on silk.

Below: explosives as entertainment. A Song emperor diverts his guests with the help of gunpowder, a chemical marvel known in China several centuries before it reached the West.

任用六賊

Homage to the past. This 13th-century terracotta of man and mount was evidently inspired by the art of the Tang, whose vigour was admired by the more refined, and perhaps effete, Song.

was already patent in the mid-11th century, when a former tributary people in the north-west, the Xia or Tangut, first asserted their independence and then went to war with China; in 1044, at the end of a four-year struggle, it was the emperor who bought peace, agreeing that the Xia, like the Khitans of Liao, should receive annual deliveries of Chinese silks and silver.

The internal problems of Song China led to the emergence of conservative and reformist factions within the ruling class. Their fortunes waxed and waned, depending on the inclinations of the emperor. The most thoroughgoing reformer was Wang Anshi, who introduced sweeping military,

administrative and fiscal changes during his tenure as chief minister between 1069 and 1076. His fiscal measures, intended to break up large estates and spread the tax burden more evenly, alienated many of the scholar-gentry, who saw their own privileges threatened. Wang advocated centralized control of commerce and transport, planned a national school system and, to the horror of traditionalists, revised the examination curriculum to give much more weight to practical problems of administration. Like other impatient reformers, Wang offended too many vested interests, making enemies even within the imperial family; he was forced to retire, and many of his measures were cancelled or allowed to lapse. His opponents were not all self-interested, but included scholars who feared that Wang's ultimate intention was to create an overbearing, autocratic state. Even now, historians are still disagreed about his character and motives.

Political debates and shifts of policy continued into the 12th century, when the Song dynasty was shaken not by internal upheavals but by powerful forces from outside. Huizong (1100–1126) was one of the most celebrated of the emperors, but for his paintings and patronage of the arts rather than his statecraft. He seems to have been in favour of enlightened reform but ennervated by his luxurious way of life and easily imposed on by self-seeking advisers. Rebellions in the 1120s suggested that the dynasty was losing support, but the emperor's downfall was brought about by a series of foreign policy blunders. The Khitan state of Liao had occupied part of North China since the mid-10th century, but by this time it was in decline; and when it came under attack from a Manchurian people, the Jurchens, the Song shortsightedly helped this rising power (not very effectively) against neighbours who no longer posed a threat. Liao was overthrown and occupied by the Jurchens, who set up a new dynasty, the Jin. Even more ill-advisedly, the Song fell out with their new allies, attacked them, and suffered a humiliating defeat. Huizong abdicated in favour of his son, but when negotiations broke down the Jin army resumed its offensive. The imperial family were trapped in Kaifeng and taken prisoners, while the Jin occupied all of China north of the river Yangtze.

One Song prince managed to escape and became the sovereign of a reduced Chinese empire which lasted for a further century and a half; it is described as the Southern Song to distinguish it from the earlier, Northern Song. For some years the Jin attempted to gain more territory, but in 1141 a treaty was signed by which the Southern Song agreed to make the usual payments; apart from two brief intervals, the treaty held for almost a hundred years, until a new power appeared in the North.

In retrospect it is tempting to view Southern Song China as a doomed remnant of empire. In

Hexagonal table of red-lacquered wood with a stone top. Furniture was sparse and mostly utilitarian in Chinese homes but, as this example shows, it was well made and strikingly designed.

reality it was a dynamic society that may well have benefited as a result of its separation from the North, which had taken resources from the South and engrossed much of the imperial attention. A decisive economic shift from North to South had already taken place. The fertile, rice-growing South supported a larger, more prosperous population than the rather bleak North; and whereas the overland routes through Central Asia had declined in importance, seaborne trade with South-East Asia, Indonesia and India was enriching the ports of the South. In the final golden age of the Song, scholarship, philosophy and the arts and crafts continued to flourish, and a sophisticated urban and commercial society developed that was at its most refined and luxurious in the capital on the east coast, Hangzhou.

One of Hangzhou's names was 'the Temporary Residence', implying a determination to recover the North and re-establish a capital there. In reality Song rulers were content to pay off the Jin and enjoy life, at least until the Mongols appeared in the North. When they did, the Song proceeded to repeat the mistakes of their predecessors: they helped the newcomers to destroy the Jin in 1233–4 and then in 1235, believing that the time was at last ripe to recover the lost territories, launched an attack on the Mongols. Since the Mongol leader, Genghis Khan, had made his name dreaded all over Asia, the Song offensive seems an inexplicably foolish act; and it did in fact lead to the destruction of the dynasty.

Victorious in East and West: a Mongol horseman with the deadly weapons that enabled Genghis Khan to build up an empire stretching from China to Poland. From an imperial Chinese seal.

MONGOL RULE

The people whom the Southern Song so recklessly attacked were the most formidable of all the nomadic tribes that traversed the Eurasian steppe, periodically descending on China and other settled civilizations. A nomad army had important military advantages: it was a mounted, mobile force, composed of men who had spent their lives in the saddle as herdsmen and hunters; consequently, they were both lethally skilful bowmen and highly disciplined warriors who were accustomed to co-ordinated action. Nomads frequently defeated the armies of the settled states, but they were weakened by tribal divisions and their way of life generally ensured that their conquests,

however swift and devastating, were impermanent. The main exception was the vast Mongol empire created by Genghis Khan, who brought all the tribes together into a single confederation (1206) and swept irresistibly across Asia from Persia to Korea. Under his successor as Great Khan, Ogodei (1227–41), Mongol armies penetrated Europe as far as Poland and Hungary. During the same period they destroyed the Jin dynasty in northern China and were attacked by the Southern Song. Thanks to distractions elsewhere, the Mongol response was relatively slow and serious offensives were only launched in the 1250s. Chinese resistance was strong, and the

Mongols' advance was hindered by the difficulties experienced by a nomad army in besieging fortified cities. But the Mongols proved surprisingly adaptable, creating a navy that matched that of the Song and taking Hangzhou in 1276 by a combined land-sea operation. Three years later the last Song resistance came to an end and for the first time the entire Chinese empire had fallen under foreign rule.

The conquest had been completed by Genghis Khan's grandson Kublai Khan, a sovereign famous in the West because Marco Polo, a Venetian merchant-traveller, took service under him and later dictated an account of his experiences that revealed the splendour of Chinese civilization to marvelling Europeans. After the death of his brother in 1259, Kublai made good his claim to be the rightful Great Khan, but his authority over distant lands ruled by independent-minded relatives was hardly secure. Recognizing China's importance as a source of wealth, Kublai moved his winter capital in 1260 to Beijing (Peking), a northern city that was inside China but not too distant from Mongolia. In 1267 he began rebuilding Beijing into the splendid city described by Marco Polo, who knew it as Cambaluc. Moreover in 1271, before Southern Song resistance had ended, Kublai had assumed the state of a Chinese emperor and proclaimed a new dynasty, the Yuan. And although China suffered during the fighting, Kublai did not allow the country to be ravaged by the Mongols, since he was shrewd enough to realize that he had more to gain by allowing its people to go on living, productive and acquiescent, in their normal fashion.

It is not easy to be sure just how acquiescent the Chinese actually were, since Kublai's rule ultimately rested on the Mongols' military power. He and his immediate successor intended that their race should remain separate from the Chinese and, in particular, should not be undermined by the pacific outlook of the conquered. Kublai and his court re-experienced the rigours of their native Mongolia each summer, and his garrisons were carefully rotated so that they did not spend too long among the temptations of the city. The Mongols remained foreigners among the

Chinese, and Marco Polo noted that the people murmured when Mongolian soldiers appeared among them. In material terms, too, the Mongol presence was burdensome, since the Chinese had to pay an extra levy, over and above the traditional taxes, to support the occupying power.

A similar ambiguity prevailed within the administrative system: the officials with whom most ordinary people came into contact were usually fellow-Chinese, but at the higher levels the government and civil service were run by foreigners. Under Kublai the service was organized in four grades. The most important positions were reserved for Mongols. At the next level outsiders were freely employed; among them were Muslim merchants and Christians, including Marco Polo himself. Confirmation that the system actually worked in this way is provided by the fact that Kublai's command of Chinese was poor, and that

Kublai Khan, grandson of the all-conquering Genghis Khan and founder of China's Yuan dynasty. Kublai's power base in China was more significant than his nominal Mongol overlordship as Great Khan.

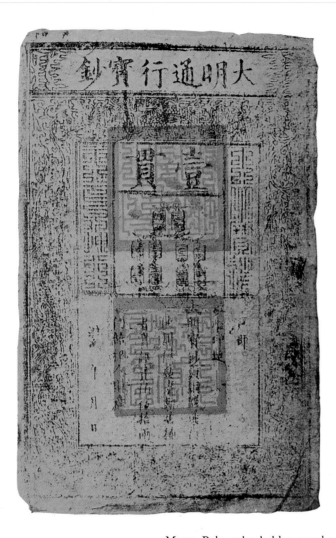

大明通行寶鈔

Banknote issued by the Mongol emperor of China, Kublai Khan. Paper money was one of the most remarkable Chinese inventions but, as the Mongols discovered, its use could have unforeseen effects.

Marco Polo, who held a number of important positions, learned to speak Mongolian but not Chinese. The third grade consisted of North Chinese, who were habituated to working for outsiders (the Khitans, the Jin, and most recently the Mongols), while the literati who had previously occupied all the posts in Southern Song China were confined to the bottom grade, performing routine tasks and receiving low salaries. The examination system was abolished and most posts were made hereditary. Later (in 1313) the examinations were restored, but discrimination continued: Mongols who passed went into the civil service two levels above Chinese who achieved the same results, while other successful foreign candidates were advantaged by one level.

Not unexpectedly, the Confucian scholar-class remained hostile to the Yuan, though its non-military traditions and lack of rapport with the common people meant that it posed no direct threat to the dynasty. Some leading Confucians

refused to serve the Mongols out of loyalty to the fallen Song and hatred of foreigners, but many less distinguished scholars, previously assured of an official post if they needed one, were simply unemployed as a result of Yuan policies. Some turned their literary skills to good use, abandoning the classical language for more popular speech forms in order to reach a non-scholarly audience. Consequently, thanks to Mongol domination, Chinese writers created the first true dramas in the language and moved towards the novel-form. Many Yuan plays, though set in the distant past, contained messages about injustice and corruption that were possibly intended to be applied to the Mongol oppressor. (Similar sentiments, even more carefully coded, were expressed in poems and paintings, but these are less likely to have had an influence on the masses.) Indirectly, at least, the pacifistic literati resisted the Yuan, and although their writings show Heaven, rather than human action, belatedly righting injustices, they are likely to have reinforced popular alienation from the regime. The importance of such influence is, of course, always conjectural.

Under Kublai, a strong, centralized administration governed China and, as in earlier times, millions of peasants were recruited to labour on a public works project on an audacious scale: an extension of the Grand Canal that ran from the Yellow River to Beijing, enabling the produce of the fertile lower Yangtze valley to be transported by water all the way to the capital, close to the north-eastern frontier.

Kublai waged war in the west, where his relatives were behaving with increasing independence. He also attempted to fulfil his destiny as the world-conquering Great Khan, launching seaborne attacks on Japan in 1274 and 1281, and penetrating South-East Asia without achieving any lasting success. Although Kublai's authority as Great Khan was limited outside China and Mongolia, relations between the Mongol khanates were usually good enough to make it relatively safe and easy to cross Asia. Taking advantage of this 'Mongol Peace', a number of Europeans, of whom Marco Polo was the most famous, managed to make their way to China. Under Kublai and his successor, Timur

Verm. Gegenst. CCCXV.

Melanges. CCCXV.

(1294–1307), Mongol rule seemed firmly established. But a series of brief, ineffectual reigns revealed the fragility of a regime that remained aloof from the people it dominated – although several emperors, unlike their fellow-Mongols, succumbed to Chinese culture and spent their time on aesthetic pursuits rather than the pursuit of power. From 1315 there were serious revolts, provoked or accompanied by natural disasters and exacerbated by a new phenomenon: galloping inflation, induced by failure to control the use of a strange Song innovation, paper money. While Mongol princes intrigued against one another, large areas of China passed out of their control. The last Yuan emperor, Toghan Timur, reigned for thirty-five years (1336–68), but could only watch impotently from his capital while Chinese factions struggled for supremacy. At last Toghan Timur fled from Beijing into Mongolia and the alien dynasty came to an end.

Kublai as field commander, directing operations from a four-elephant mobile headquarters. Whether fact or fantasy, the image of a mighty military machine is entirely appropriate.

RADIANT DYNASTY

During the final thirty years of the Yuan era, the wars between rebel Chinese groups were in many ways more momentous than the struggle against the enfeebled Mongols. A key role was played by the Red Turbans, a messianic sect of the type that often appeared in China during times of crisis. Though disappointed in their expectation that the Maitreya – the Buddha of the Future – was about to appear, the Red Turbans did produce one of history's more remarkable military and political leaders. By birth Zhu Yuanzhang was scarcely a member of Chinese society. As an orphan child he had escaped starvation by joining a Buddhist monastery. In 1355, three years after joining a local Red Turban group, he became its leader and immediately showed his ability by capturing the city of Nanjing, which became his headquarters and capital. He soon became the protector of the Red Turban claimant to the Dragon Throne, who died in a convenient accident, leaving the way open for Zhu himself to become the candidate. A naval victory at Boyang Lake (1363) disposed of his main rival, but five years of fighting and consolidation were needed before Zhu became undisputed master of China. In 1368 he proclaimed himself the first emperor of the Ming ('radiant') dynasty. In the West he is generally known by the laudatory title given to his reign, Hongwu (military might).

Hongwu (1368–98) proved to be strong and successful, but also a tyrant with no inhibitions about shedding blood. He worked hard to restore order and prosperity in the countryside, creating a sound local government structure and improving irrigation. Many of his measures revived traditional customs and institutions, setting the prevailing tone of Ming China, which was to be increasingly inward-looking, traditionalist and antiquarian. But politically the Ming emperors were the heirs of the Mongols rather than earlier dynasties. Following Hongwu's example, they ruled as unbridled autocrats, impatient of older forms and restraints. A number of leading ministerial posts at court were abolished, giving the emperor more direct control over the army and the administration. Since not only the ministers but their secretaries were dispensed with, this had the drawback of imposing a heavy burden on the emperor; the hyperactive Hongwu coped with it, but many of the frailer or less conscientious rulers who succeeded him inevitably neglected their duties or left the business of making decisions to palace favourites.

From Hongwu's reign the influence of the Confucian literati was severely curtailed, and the licence previously granted to the scholar-official to criticize his sovereign's actions could only be exercised at some personal risk. Arbitrary violence on the part of the emperors became common under the Ming, following the example of the founding emperor. Perhaps all too conscious of his humble origins, Hongwu displayed an attitude towards his higher officials that smacks of paranoia, ordering mass executions of suspects and their families, in a fashion worthy of his Qin predecessor some 1,600 years earlier; in seeking out and eliminating the remotest relatives of just one fallen minister, the emperor is calculated to have put to death a staggering 40,000 people.

Opposite: Hongwu, first emperor of the Ming ('radiant') dynasty. Thanks to his energetic, if ruthless, policies, the dynasty ruled China for almost 300 years, from 1368 to 1644.

Left: pottery figure of a bodhisattva, an enlightened being who remains on earth to help humanity. By Ming times Buddhism had become thoroughly integrated into the Chinese way of life.

Although some officials continued to give the emperors good but unwelcome advice and suffered for it, in government, as in other areas of Ming life, an atmosphere of conformism became increasingly prevalent.

Like many autocrats, Hongwu was led into error by his partiality for his own family. His twenty-six sons were given titles and territories which could easily be converted into war-lord-

ships, with all the obvious dangers to the state that such 'feudal' arrangements always hold. Fortunately for the Ming, the crisis occurred early in the dynasty and was successfully resolved. When Hongwu died after a thirty-year reign, he was succeeded by his twenty-one-year-old grandson, Jianwen (1398–1402), who realized the threat posed by his uncles and worked to reduce their power. Early in his reign he clashed with

uneasiness which caused him to send out hordes of agents at home and abroad on the (almost certainly non-existent) trail of his fallen rival.

Frustration and fear probably explained the savage purge that followed Yongle's accession: every possible rival and every prominent supporter of Jianwen was executed, along with their families to remote degrees of relationship. But after his initial excesses Yongle showed himself to be a highly capable sovereign, strengthening the state (and protecting himself against usurpers who proposed to imitate his bad example) by ensuring that members of the imperial clan were not allowed to build up large military followings. Though the numbers, titles and lands of the Ming clan steadily increased over the centuries (eventually constituting a burden on the economy), they were never again a serious military threat to the imperial throne.

Like any leader, Yongle needed a certain amount of luck, which in his case manifested itself in a negative event: he was not compelled to face the latest of the great nomad conquerors, Timur or Tamerlaine, who died in 1405 when his horde was poised to invade China. As a result, Yongle figures in history as a successful military man, occupying Vietnam and inflicting severe defeats on the Mongols. Even so, the northern border remained a matter of constant concern, as the emperor recognized in 1421 when he transferred the Ming capital from Nanjing to Beijing in the north, from which he could respond quickly to any threatening developments. The rebuilding and expansion of Beijing followed, and it was under the Ming that it began to take on its now-famous form and atmosphere as the imperial 'Forbidden City'.

Under Yongle, China was once more the greatest and wealthiest power in Asia. Outlying regions, notably Sichuan, Yunnan and Guizhou in the south-west, were incorporated into the empire, and so (for the time being) was Vietnam. Official missions were repeatedly sent out and made contact with the Mongols, the cities of Central Asia, the South-East Asian kingdoms and Japan. The commercial relations that ensued were interpreted by the emperors in self-flattering terms: the barbarians sent tribute to the Son of

Hongwu's fourth son, the Duke of Yen, who had already proved himself an energetic commander in defending his lands, which lay on the northeast frontier. Realizing his nephew's intentions, the Duke led a revolt that was ultimately successful and became emperor as Yongle. Jianwen appeared to have perished when his palace burned down, but there was no identifiable corpse and the usurping Yongle suffered from a constant

Left: the formidable walls, towers and fortifications of the Great Wall of China. Already 1,500 years old when the Ming began to rule the empire, the Great Wall was given essentially its present appearance by the dynasty.

Heaven, who responded to their submission with graciously bestowed gifts. In some cases this was no more than a satisfying fiction, but politics and commerce were certainly intertwined in the astonishing seafaring feats of Admiral Zheng He. Between 1405 and 1433 Zheng He, 'the three-jewelled eunuch', made seven voyages in the waters of the Indian ocean, visiting the coastal states of southern Asia, the Persian Gulf and East Africa. His huge fleet of ocean-going junks carried tens of thousands of men, so that there was an element of intimidation in its descent which made advisable the opening of diplomatic relations and trade/tribute transactions accompanied by an acceptance of Chinese suzerainty; and in fact Zheng He occasionally found it necessary to use force when recalcitrant potentates (one was the king of Sri Lanka) were taken prisoner and made the long voyage to China in chains. Since the countries concerned were far away from the Middle Kingdom, their submission was not much more than a formality, but the Chinese expeditions were nonetheless brilliant demonstrations of the empire's power and wealth.

The belief that all other peoples were (or ought to have been) tributaries restricted Chinese appreciation of the world beyond the Middle Kingdom, but Zheng He's voyages suggested that the Ming might after all become more outward-looking. However, after Yongle's death, the trend was decisively reversed. The Chinese were expelled with humiliating completeness from Vietnam, Zheng He was permitted to make only one more voyage (1431–3), and renewed Mongol activity helped to create a defensive rather than expansive mentality. The reappearance of eunuchs as a political force has also been blamed for the troubles that afflicted the dynasty, although the alternative ruling elite – the scholar-bureaucrat class – was at least as likely to take up conservative and inward-looking attitudes. After all, it was the eunuch Zheng He who led the great seaborne expeditions, and although the reason why they were discontinued is not entirely clear, there is little doubt about the anti-foreign and anti-mercantile attitude of the Confucian officials. Once the decision to discontinue the voyages had been taken, there was never

any question of reversing it; no more large sea-going vessels were built, and around 1480, as though they contained black-magical temptations, all the records of Zheng He's journeys were destroyed. In the long run this rejection of the outside world would prove to be a tragic error.

Although some eunuchs were able and disinterested servants of the dynasty, there were inevitably intriguers who won promotion by exploiting their special position as palace officials; and perhaps because of the fragile nature of their power, they often exercised it recklessly and brutally. The first Ming emperor, aware of their potentially dangerous influence, decreed that eunuchs should be restricted to domestic service and not be taught to read. But the support of the palace eunuchs helped Yongle to the Dragon Throne, and during his reign they acquired a strong influence that got out of hand in later reigns, especially when the sovereign was young and easily led.

Ultimately, of course, the fault lay in a system that depended so completely on the character of a single individual. Under Xuande (1425–35),

despite military reverses, good government in the Confucian mould prevailed; the Son of Heaven himself became renowned for an unimperial inclination towards clemency, and some harsh judicial punishments were replaced by the payment of fines. But when the emperor was succeeded by his seven-year-old son, Ying Zong (1435–49, 1457–64), Wang Zheng became the first of several eunuchs who intermittently exercised dictatorial powers at the Ming court.

Wang Zheng's predominance coincided with (and perhaps hastened) a serious decline in the authority of the government, which failed to restrain the growing power of the landlord class, raised taxes without managing to strengthen the administration or the army, and by the 1440s found itself faced with the combination of popular risings and natural disasters that usually signalled the approaching end of the dynasty. And worse was to follow. Wang Zheng's career ended when he was killed at Tumubao, having launched the still-young emperor on a campaign for which the Chinese army was ill-prepared. The emperor was taken prisoner and the Mongols pressed

Scholars gathering in a bamboo garden; 15th-century painting on silk. Cultivated Chinese were unusual in combining a passion for learning with a sensitive pleasure in the natural world.

south, apparently less interested in conquest than in selling the emperor back to his subjects – who, however, wrong-footed their foes by elevating Ying Zong's brother to the Dragon Throne.

Surprisingly, the dynasty survived, even though the Mongols released the now-valueless Ying Zong, presumably in the hope that the existence of rival emperors would plunge China into civil war; instead, Ying Zong bided his time and, seven years after his deposition, regained power in a palace coup and reigned until his death in 1464. The long-term result of the 1449 disaster was to concentrate attention yet again on the northern frontier. Thinking primarily in defensive terms, the Chinese pinned their faith on the 1,500-year-old Great Wall, which had formerly separated the Middle Kingdom in very definite fashion from the nomad-dominated lands to the north. The wall had already been substantially repaired by Hongwu; his operations, along with the work put in hand by the later Ming emperors, gave the wall the formidable appearance it has had ever since. (Whether it was militarily effective is another matter.) The Great Wall that the modern visitor sees is not the Qin emperor's creation, but essentially its re-creation, in stone and along a somewhat different line, by the Ming.

From the mid-15th century the history of the dynasty was chequered, in part because of its mortality rate: most of the emperors came to the throne as teenagers, each dying early enough in life to leave behind an equally youthful heir. One exceptional figure was Hongzhi (1487–1505), who became emperor at seventeen but became widely regarded as a model sovereign in the approved Confucian style. His predecessor and most of his successors were less capable, allowing others to rule them or asserting themselves mainly to indulge expensive caprices; both were true of Zhengde (1505–21), whose vices were encouraged by one of the ruthless, power-seeking eunuchs who figured increasingly in the political struggles of the period. Zhengde's successor, Jiajing (1521–67), took up the ancient Daoist quest for the Elixir of Life, surviving the potions he imbibed and enjoying a respectably long reign.

The fortunes of the political elite are not always a reliable guide to the general condition of

a society, and Ming China was notably prosperous during the late 15th century and for much of the 16th. The peasants benefited from the application of improved agricultural techniques and an increase in the acreage under cultivation, especially when the imperial authorities reformed the

A busy street scene in a Ming town. Most Chinese lived on the land, but the population was so enormous that cities were thronged and offered a wide variety of services and pleasures.

tax system and checked the worst abuses of local power by landowners. The tax reforms were mainly a matter of simplifying and consolidating payments, a process known (by an untranslatable pun) as the Single Whip system. This was made easier by the growth of a money economy stimu-lated by silver payments from abroad and the flourishing state of trade.

There were also positive developments in learning and the arts. Official culture may have been narrow in its outlook, but its scholarly achievements were impressive. An enormous

The Jesuit missionary Matteo Ricci dressed as a Confucian scholar. This 'wise man from the West' successfully bridged two civilizations, using his scientific knowledge to help the Chinese, but also mastering the language and culture of his hosts.

compendium of all existing knowledge was researched and published on the orders of Yongle, and later authors compiled pioneering encyclopaedias of medicine and technology. These and many other works were widely circulated through printing, and widely read thanks to the excellent system of education. The first Chinese novels were written during the Ming period, and the literati painter-poet-calligraphers developed new styles; many lived in retirement, far from the court and its more assertive art and architecture, which are still visible in the Forbidden City and the statue-lined grand avenue that leads to the imperial tombs. Of the industrial arts, its exquisite porcelain was to make the Ming famous all over the world.

When Admiral Zheng He's expeditions ended, ship-building languished and there was a decline in Chinese interest in the outer regions beyond the Middle Kingdom. The ocean abandoned by the Ming was penetrated by Portuguese caravels, followed by the ships of other European nations. In 1511 the Portuguese captured Malacca, formerly a tributary which Zheng He had used as the base from which he set out on his expeditions. Three years later the Portuguese became the first Europeans to reach China by sea in their own ships. The Chinese did not realize the momentous nature of the event, and an official Portuguese envoy who arrived in 1517 was not allowed to go forward to Beijing until 1520 – when he was not granted an audience and, after Portuguese crews misbehaved, was thrown into prison and remained there until his death. The Portuguese were eventually allowed to settle at Macao and trade with China, and other European vessels began to arrive. So did Christian missionaries, including the Jesuit Matteo Ricci, whose mastery of the Chinese language and the Confucian classics earned him the respect of scholars; his knowledge of astronomy enabled him to correct the calendar, but it was a technological marvel presented to the emperor – a striking clock – that secured his position. Later Jesuits used their scientific knowledge to help the Ming in casting cannons, despite which the Chinese failed to appreciate the fact – or at any rate the importance of the fact – that they were beginning to fall behind the distant western barbarians in a number of fields. Accounts of China sent back by Ricci and others, along with shipments of Chinese merchandise, made a strong impression on Europeans; but China was hardly touched as yet by contact with the West.

The emperor who was so delighted by Ricci's clock was Wanli (1572–1620), during whose reign Chinese society went into a rapid decline. The first ten years seemed promising, since Wanli was still a child and power was exercised by the able Zhang Juzheng. This minister strengthened the defences and introduced some reforms, notably the phasing out of paper money; however useful in principle, this confidence-based currency had proved too much for Chinese governments to handle and had occasioned alarming bursts of inflation. But after Zhang Juzheng's

death in 1582, the court became riddled with intrigues, as the emperor strove to install as his heir his son by a favourite concubine, while his advisers doggedly championed the empress's son. Though Wanli was capable of lashing out at anyone who criticized him directly, he was too weak-minded to resist sustained pressure from the bureaucracy, whose candidate was eventually designated as his successor.

Later on, the emperor's bizarre behaviour resulted in the near-paralysis of the imperial administration. Whether through pique or growing eccentricity, Wanli grew increasingly unwilling to make contact with his own officials, taking a perverse delight in slipping away, disappointing their expectations, refusing to make appointments and in other ways deliberately holding up the business of government. This was all the more serious because the general situation was deteriorating. Though elusive, Wanli was extravagant, and vast sums were spent on ceremonial occasions and rebuilding the Forbidden City, which was badly damaged by fire in 1596 and again in 1597. Neglect of the army and the virtual scrapping of the navy turned new Mongol wars and persistent Japanese piracy into crises. And the first challenge to Chinese predominance in East Asia occurred when the Japanese invaded Korea and their leader, Hideyoshi Toyotomi, boasted that this was the first step in the conquest of China itself. Large Chinese forces were despatched to help the Koreans, and after several campaigns (1592–7) the Japanese were forced to withdraw. But the effort exhausted the Chinese exchequer, and the imposition of new and heavy taxes was ominously answered by the outbreak of revolts.

The imperial regime surmounted the immediate crisis, but the accession of yet another extravagant, incompetent youth, and the rise of another eunuch dictator, intensified discontent. Epidemics and famines hastened the end. From the late 1620s large areas of China were occupied by rebel armies. Finally, in 1644 the most successful leader, Li Zicheng, marched on Beijing. The imperial generals failed to come to the rescue, and when the rebel troops entered the city, the last Ming emperor withdrew to a hill overlooking his palaces and hanged himself.

The Emperor Kangxi reigned from 1669 to 1722, during which time he consolidated the Manchu hold on China. This alien dynasty was China's last imperial line.

THE MANCHUS

While Ming China imploded, a new force was gathering strength in the north-east. The Manchus were mainly descendants of the Jurchen tribes which had overthrown the Northern Song five centuries earlier and had set up the Jin dynasty. Scattered over the north-east, the Manchus were united by two remarkable leaders, Nurhaci and Abahai; they created a territorial administration, installed a Chinese-style bureaucracy and organized their warriors and officials into military-administrative groups, each with its own banner. As more and more groups north of the Great Wall came under Manchu control, Chinese and Mongols were also organized into units of bannermen. Large numbers of Chinese proved willing to take service with the Manchus, who had by this time adopted Confucian values and other features of the Chinese way of life, almost as though preparing for a prominent role within the empire itself.

As early as 1618 the Manchus launched an attack on China, but their expansion elsewhere (including Korea, traditionally part of the Chinese sphere of influence) provided the empire with a respite from which it failed to profit. In the mid-1630s Abahai changed the name of his people from Jurchens to Manchus, and declared himself emperor, taking the dynastic name Qing ('Pure'); in effect he was asserting a claim to become the new sovereign of the Middle Kingdom, whose Ming rulers had clearly forfeited the Mandate of Heaven.

Abahai died in 1643, but Manchu leadership under his child-successor was assumed by Dorjon, a regent who was both able and loyal. This was fortunate for the Manchus, whose great opportunity came only a year later. When the Ming emperor died and the rebel Li Zicheng entered Beijing in triumph, the forces of the Chinese general Wu Sangui were bivouacked not far to the north, within the Great Wall. Since an attack by the rebels was imminent, Wu Sangui made an alliance with the Manchus, who entered China with unconscious symbolism through the great gateway known as The First Entrance Under Heaven. Wu Sangui may have acted initially as a Ming loyalist, prepared to destroy rebels with the aid of the barbarians, who could then be paid off or expelled with the assistance of other imperial forces. Or the general may himself have had imperial ambitions which made it imperative to eliminate Li Zicheng, who had already proclaimed himself the first emperor of the Shu dynasty.

If either of these was his motive, the general miscalculated badly. Li Zincheng was duly

The Buddhist paradise; 17th-century painting. The Manchu conquerors of China were followers of the Lamaist (Tibetan) school of Buddhism, which increased its already growing influence.

despatched, but the Manchus proceeded to occupy Beijing and their seven-year-old ruler became the Shunzhi emperor (1644–61). Wu Sangui and other generals quickly fell into line and marched south to quell Ming pretenders and carve out principalities for themselves. And so the last imperial dynasty, the Qing, was a foreign one. Paradoxically, these outsiders would restore and expand the frontiers of China, giving the state its present vast dimensions; but in time these same outsiders would, despite their martial qualities, come to epitomize China's weakness and backwardness, to such an extent that, when they fell, they brought down the entire imperial system with them. All of this lay far in the future. During

A provincial governor exercising his authority. This English engraving was published in 1690 as part of an account describing early contacts with China. Establishing normal diplomatic relations with the Celestial Empire proved frustratingly difficult.

its first four decades, the dynasty looked quite vulnerable. Its writ hardly ran in the South, where three Chinese generals, operating as agents of the Qing, built up powerful fiefs in the process of eliminating the remaining pockets of Ming support. Fortunately for the Qing, the generals or 'feudatories' remained quiescent until the dynasty seemed inclined to re-assert imperial control. The strongest of the generals, Wu Sangui, revolted in 1673, almost thirty years after he had opened The First Entrance Under Heaven to the Manchus. By this time the dynasty was secure in the North and the empire was being ruled by one of the most spectacularly successful of all Chinese emperors, Kangxi (1661–1722). Even so, 'the Revolt of the Three Feudatories' was a severe test of the Qing, and for a time before his death in 1678 Wu Sangui came close to overthrowing the dynasty. Many parts of the South were devastated before the last resistance was crushed in 1681. Land-sea operations were also undertaken against the piratical allies of the feudatories, leading on in 1683 to the first Chinese occupation of the very large neighbouring island of Taiwan.

Having stabilized the political situation, the Manchus were much more successful than their Mongol predecessors in securing Chinese acceptance of their rule and the willing co-operation of the official class. Even in their homeland, the Manchus had adopted the Chinese way of life, and large numbers of Chinese had entered the Qing army and administration even before the breach-ing of the Great Wall; for example, eight of the twenty-four 'banners' were Chinese, a fact that must have reduced any racial antagonism towards the banners' privileged position within the empire. As a security measure, most senior military and administrative posts were held by Manchus, in some cases alongside Chinese officials. This did mean a relative shortage of jobs for the most gifted graduates from the examination system, occasioning some discontent. But at the middle and lower levels the officials and magistrates were Chinese, essentially no different from those that the peasants had dealt with for centuries. The Manchus learned to speak Chinese as well as the natives, and when Qing emperors addressed the people, they did so in the approved, high-minded Confucian fashion.

However, the 'normality' established by the Qing had its limits. The Manchus retained their own language as well as learning Chinese, and in important matters of appearance it was the Chinese who were compelled to change. The Manchu shaved forehead and pigtail, de rigeur for all their subjects, were resented as visible symbols of foreign domination; significantly, almost the first act of any rebel was to cut off his pigtail. Despite their adoption of Chinese culture, the Manchus maintained their separate identity, and their Manchurian homeland remained an independent state with its own capital at Mukden. The early Qing emperors made strenuous efforts to impress their Chinese subjects with their Confucian virtues, but they also spent their summers in Inner Mongolia, hunting and shooting in order to preserve their Manchu (and certainly non-Confucian) physical vigour. Nor were the banners integrated into Chinese society; on the theory that participation in agriculture or commerce would erode their martial skills and spirits, they were retained as a subsidized elite, the predictable result being . . . the erosion of their martial skills and spirits.

If the record of the Manchus' dealings with their Chinese subjects was a mixed one, it proved good enough to sustain the imperial regime, at least in prosperous times. And from the late 17th century, when the worst effects of the invasion and civil wars had passed, Qing China enjoyed a great surge of prosperity. Driven on by renewed population growth after the disasters of the Ming era, farmers broke new lands and introduced new techniques and crops. The authorities assisted the process by lowering agricultural taxes and remitting them altogether in war-ravaged areas.

This general prosperity, lasting well into the 18th century, was made possible because China was ruled by a series of emperors who carried out their duties conscientiously and avoided the worst imperial excesses of favouritism, corruption and tyrannical caprice. Kangxi's reputation for shrewdness is exemplified by the stratagem he is said to have used to win over literati who remained loyal to the Ming. He appointed them to the board of scholars charged with compiling a history of the fallen dynasty; they could hardly refuse such a pious task and, once in salaried employment under the Qing, found that working for the new regime was tolerable and even habit-forming. Many other scholars were not hostile but simply jobless, and Kangxi was careful to make provision for them by patronizing encyclopaedic and similarly labour-intensive literary projects. This reinforced the image the emperor wished to create, of a Confucian scholar-sovereign rather than a Manchu outsider; as early as 1670 he issued a set of Sacred Edicts, in effect a Confucian Sixteen Commandments in which virtues such as filial piety and punctual payment of taxes were extolled. Later on, Kangxi innovated by making eleven tours of his dominions which seem to have combined business with pleasure in a highly effective fashion: the emperor was seen by his people, inspected irrigation and similar projects, discussed local affairs with the officials most closely in touch with them, and saw the sights. Combined with his palace-based information network, kept separate from the official bureaucracy, such activities made Kangxi a singularly well-informed sovereign with a realistic grasp of Chinese conditions.

Coming to the throne as a child, Kangxi assumed power in 1669 at the early age of fifteen. Consequently he was already in control during the Revolt of the Three Feudatories, as well as coping with later diplomatic and military problems. The most important of these were threats from the north and north-west. In the early 17th century, Russian prospectors, traders and settlers surged across Siberia, all the way to the Pacific; they were followed in short order by the Tsar's soldiers, who built a fort within Chinese territory and attempted to dominate or win over northern tribes that had previously paid tribute to the Qing. Kangxi tolerated Russian encroachments until the Revolt of the Three Feudatories had been successfully dealt with, but then he undertook a campaign which destroyed most of the Russian settlements and prompted the Russians to seek peace. In making the treaty of Nerchinsk (1689), the Chinese were assisted by Jesuit missionaries, who were able to advise them on the niceties of European diplomacy. The outcome was a treaty between equals, something hitherto unknown to sovereigns raised to believe that the only legitimate relationship between the Middle Kingdom and other peoples was that of suzerain and tribute-bearers.

The Chinese had acquitted themselves well in their first significant encounter with the forces of a European power. The Russians withdrew from the contested areas, gaining in return the right to send trade caravans to Beijing. Both sides had an interest in making peace, since both feared that they might otherwise face a coalition of their enemies. The third force in northern Asia was the Western Mongol or Zunghar people, who had built up a formidable steppe empire and pressed hard on the Mongolian lands north of the Great Wall, which had become Chinese tributary states. Having made peace with Russia, Kangxi responded to the next Zunghar attack by personally leading a large army against them. In the campaigns of 1696–7 they were thoroughly defeated and their chief, Galdan, perished. They were not yet broken, but they offered no serious threat to China for a generation.

In his last years Kangxi's judgement became less certain, and his refusal to name a successor added to the tensions of the period. It was widely rumoured that the sixty-six-year-old emperor was murdered by his fourth son, Yongzheng (1723–35), although the rumours may only have been generated by the speed and efficiency with which Yongzheng seized the opportunity offered

by his father's death and disabled his rivals. The new emperor reduced the power of the imperial clan, and his often harshly autocratic methods stamped out the corruption that had begun to infect the system towards the end of Kangxi's reign. Wiser than his father, Yongzheng named his successor; but he kept his decision a secret, written down but locked away until he had died. Later emperors followed his example, since this simple device avoided a contested succession but did not encourage the plotting to which impatience might have tempted a prince who knew for

A view of the Qing imperial court at Beijing. It gives some idea of the ceremonial splendour of life in the Forbidden City, in which an emperor could all too easily become a pampered prisoner.

certain that he was the designated heir. Yongzheng left a secure throne and a prosperous empire to his son Qianlong, whose very long reign (1736–96) has often been described as the high point of Chinese greatness. In many respects Qianlong modelled himself on his grandfather Kangxi. He rose early, consulted with his ministers every day, set himself to absorb the administrative details, diligently read the classics and made tours of inspection through the provinces. Benefiting from the long internal peace, Chinese agriculture and commerce flourished. Food supplies sustained the court, administration and army, and even seemed capable of satisfying a population that was increasing at an alarming speed. In 1660 there were probably about 120 million Chinese, but their numbers may well have declined steeply during the Qing invasion, the wars against the Ming pretenders and the long and bloody Revolt of the Three Feudatories. Nevertheless the Chinese census for 1762 showed that the figure had risen to 200 million, and within sixty years it had almost doubled.

In territorial extent the Chinese empire reached its zenith at the end of the 1750s. The troublesome Zunghars were destroyed in a series of brutal campaigns whose outcome can be described without exaggeration as genocide. Their momentum carried the Chinese armies further west, and they reduced to submission a huge area which was later known as Xinjiang (Sinkiang), the New Territories; though kept under military government for a century, it eventually became (and remains) a province of China. The elimination of the Zunghars, who had adhered to the Tibetan form of Buddhism, made it possible for the Chinese to make good their claim to be the paramount power in Tibet itself, ending a long period of ambiguity. As a result, China reached its greatest extent ever, controlling not only the present-day territories of the People's Republic, but Mongolia ('Outer' Mongolia) and large areas later ceded to Russia. China dominated East Asia, whose states acknowledged its

suzerainty and sent envoys with tributes to Beijing. Like many long-lived autocrats, Qianlong became insulated from realities in his later years and allowed the quality of his administration to decline. His vanity, ill-disguised even in his mature proclamations, seems to have become even more pronounced in old age. Formerly the munificent patron of scholarship and literature, he mounted a campaign in the 1770s to destroy any writings that contained criticism of the Manchus or the behaviour of the authorities present or past; more than 2,000 books are believed to have perished over a period of fifteen years although, as in the Qin burning almost 2,000 years earlier, many proved to have survived in copies hidden by devout bibliophiles. Shortly afterwards Qianlong committed a greater folly, making a favourite of an attractive young man named He Shen, who acquired almost every available high office and a complete ascendancy over the emperor. Though not without ability, He Shen was greedy and corrupt. Favours and offices were sold at the highest possible price, and since the buyers needed to recoup their heavy investments, a similar corruption spread through the administration and much of the army.

Inevitably the people at the bottom of the social pyramid – the peasants – suffered the worst exploitation. Their miseries may already have been exacerbated by the effects of rising population on limited resources. Not for the first time, popular discontent was mobilized by the leaders of millenarian religious sects that promised an end to suffering and a new material and spiritual order. There were a number of outbreaks from the 1770s onwards, but the severest challenge occurred in the 1790s with the revolt of the White Lotus sect, whose leaders preached that the coming of the Maitreya Buddha (the Buddha of the Future) was imminent.

During the later part of Qianlong's reign the quality of the bannermen declined, but mediocre performances against the Burmese and Vietnamese appeared to have been redeemed in 1792 by a victorious campaign in Tibet against the Gurkhas which reduced Nepal to tributary status. However the failure of repeated attempts to put down the White Lotus rebellion demon-

A Qing interior of the late 18th century, with the living space divided up by partitions. Its traditional sparseness is relieved by restrained decoration and the use of well-chosen objets d'art.

Chinese labourers working a tread-device to transfer water from the river to their fields; watercolour by William Alexander (1767–1816), a British artist who accompanied Lord Macartney's 1793 embassy.

strated that real weaknesses existed in the direction and execution of military policies. The rebellion lasted for eight years and might have gone on longer if there had not been a change of regime. In 1796 Qianlong, much addicted to gestures that affirmed his Confucian credentials, abdicated rather than reign longer than his revered grandfather; but he continued to rule – or rather to let He Shen rule – behind the scenes.

Qianlong died in 1799 and his son Jiaqing (1796–1820) became the actual as well as the nominal sovereign. He Shen was graciously permitted to take his own life, and his ill-gotten gains (at 80 million taels about twice the annual income of the treasury) were returned to the imperial coffers. Vigorously concerted measures were taken against the White Lotus rebels, who were gradually driven back and destroyed.

Jiaqing reduced court expenditure and introduced a number of reforms. But China's economic difficulties were not easily solved and peasant discontent continued to simmer. At one point in 1813 the Three Trigrams Rebellion put the dynasty in serious danger when followers of a revived White Lotus sect initiated but bungled a daring coup attempt in the Forbidden City itself. Under Jiaqing and his son Dao Guang (1821–50), peasant and ethnic minority rebellions multiplied. They were successfully put down, but each one weakened the regime and suggested that the Qing might not possess the Mandate of Heaven for much longer.

CONFRONTING THE WEST

'The Reception of an English Envoy at the Court of Peking'. This irreverent view of Macartney's embassy, by the satirist James Gillray, is characteristically mocking of both parties.

In the long history of imperial China, the decline of the Qing might have signified nothing more than a change of dynasty. The familiar patterns of vigour and decadence, rigour and relapse, could have continued without uprooting traditional Chinese civilization. But the dynastic cycle was disrupted, and the civilization changed for ever, by the intervention of foreign powers, stronger than any Chinese imagined and increasingly determined to breach the enclosed world of the Middle Kingdom.

By the Qing period, no traces remained of the cosmopolitanism of the Tang. Foreigners were regarded by the authorities as tedious beings whose proper willingness to pay tribute must be tolerated, but whose visits must be brief and closely supervised. Jesuit missionaries had made some impression because they brought with them ingenious devices (striking clocks) and a mastery of such useful subjects as mathematics and astronomy. Kangxi favoured them for a time, and the Jesuits made converts by interpreting Confucian ancestor-veneration as a social rather than religious custom, which Chinese Christians could be allowed to keep up. When the Vatican ruled against tolerating 'the Rites', the emperor was alienated and Christian influence declined, though some covert missionary work carried on.

In the 16th century, Portuguese vessels reached China and sought opportunities to trade. Bribery gained them the use of Macao as a base, but the Portuguese and the nationalities that followed their example found China more formidable to deal with than most African and Asian societies they encountered. Instead of imposing their will and setting up mini-states from which to trade and perhaps conquer, European merchants operated within strictly defined limits. From 1760 all European maritime trade was chanelled through a single port, Canton, and processed by a handful of Chinese merchants belonging to a special guild, the Cohong; the situation reflected Chinese notions of collective responsibility, making the guild liable for any bad behaviour on the part of its members or the foreign merchants with whom they did business. To Europeans the actions of the Chinese authorities often seemed high-handed and unjust, but they were even more vexed by their limited opportunities to ship Chinese tea, silks and porcelain to eager buyers in the West. Nor were they able to sell significant amounts of merchandise to the Chinese; and as a result everything they wanted had to be paid for in silver, which was shipped from West to East in alarming quantities.

By the late 18th century Britain was visibly the greatest European power in the East, mainly thanks to the government-licensed British East India Company, which had developed into a mercantile and political force that dominated much of India. In an attempt to establish some kind of official relationship with China, the Company and the British government jointly sponsored a lavishly equipped embassy to Qianlong, led by Lord George Macartney. As usual, the Chinese interpreted the visit as a humble tribute-bearing. Macartney was escorted to Beijing and, although he refused to perform the kowtow (the ritual prostration in front of the emperor), was admitted to Qianlong's presence. But his requests for greater freedom of trade and British diplomatic representation in China were met with polite indifference and no further dialogue was permitted. Macartney returned to Britain with a letter to George III in which Qianlong made it clear that increased trade was out of the question, since Britain possessed nothing of which the Celestial Empire had the slightest need. A later attempt to establish relations by Lord Amherst (1815) was less ceremoniously rebuffed.

Unlike the imperial government, many Chinese traders were eager to engage in commerce, legal or otherwise, with the foreigner. By the 1770s the East India Company had realized that the flow of silver into China could be stemmed by trading in a commodity cultivated in British India: the drug opium. Exports to China increased with a satisfying rapidity, from about

A more solemn view of Britain's first embassy to China than Gillray's (opposite). Qianlong's retinue approaches the imperial tent to receive Macartney; engraving by William Alexander.

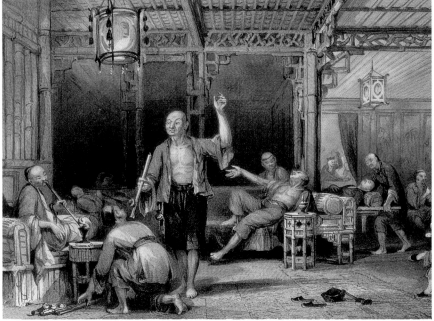

Top: an elegant, late 19th-century opium set. The main source of opium was British India, and when the Chinese authorities sought to cut off supplies, the British were prepared to go to war.

Above: engraving by Thomas Allom, expressing the 19th-century British view of Chinese opium smokers. Moral disapproval did not prevent Britain from promoting huge sales of the drug to China.

1,000 chests a year in the 1770s to over 5,000 in 1816, despite imperial bans on importing, and finally on smoking, the drug.

Fifteen years later the figure had quadrupled, and addiction and an unfavourable balance of payments were adding to the problems of a struggling dynasty. Advisers at the imperial court disputed whether it would be more effective to legalize the drug or attempt to make the prohibitions effective. In 1838 Emperor Dao Guang decided on an all-out campaign against opium and appointed a special commissioner to carry it out. Commissioner Lin Zexu acted with admirable vigour, combining police raids with Confucian exhortation in an attempt to clean up Canton. His faith in the power of reason led him to send a letter to Queen Victoria, appealing to her sense of honour; but he also instructed the for-

eign merchants to hand over their stockpiles of opium. After a standoff during which the foreign community in Canton was blockaded but not attacked, 20,000 chests of opium were handed over and destroyed under the personal supervision of Lin Zexu.

Unfortunately Lin's triumph did not solve the problem of addiction and could not be sustained in the face of political realities. The British government sent a fleet to punish the insult to its subjects and obtain compensation. It arrived in June 1840, and although confused negotiating positions on both sides prolonged the conflict, there was never any serious doubt about the overwhelming technological superiority of the British. Shanghai was captured and the Yangtze blockaded. When British forces invested Nanjing, the Qing sued for peace. The Treaty of Nanjing (1842) opened five ports to the British, who were permitted to reside there and trade with whomsoever they pleased; consulates could also be established. The Chinese ceded the island of Hong Kong to Britain and paid an indemnity and compensation for the destroyed opium stock. The United States, France and other western states were swift to secure equivalent and even extended rights for themselves. Rapidly expanding, the foreign mercantile settlements in China became privileged, effectively sovereign enclaves, known as 'concessions'.

The Qing adapted in a half-hearted fashion, still believing that, like barbarians in the past, the westerners would in time weaken and disappear. The improvised responses of the imperial government seem more reasonable in the light of its internal problems. As public works deteriorated and the bureaucracy became increasingly corrupt, China was beginning to seem ungovernable; and then, against this background of general disorder, the Qing faced a severe challenge from a new and bizarre sect: the Taiping.

The founder of the Taiping was a failed scholar, Hong Xiuquan, who came into contact with Protestant missionaries and became convinced by a vision that he was the younger son of Jesus Christ. Gathering converts in the poor province of Guanxi, Hong's movement seemed no more than a nuisance in 1850; but then a series of

victories over Qing troops along the Yangtze culminated in the capture of Nanjing, traditionally China's 'southern capital', in 1853, and the massacre of tens of thousands of Manchus. The Taiping remained a major force for a further eleven years, but they failed to make significant progress and were weakened by murderous infighting among the leaders and a limited appeal. They were not only anti-Manchu but anti-Confucian, burning temples and forbidding ancestral rites wherever they took control. Their stance meant that few of the influential scholar-gentry class rallied to them; and in fact, feeling their fundamental values under threat, Chinese officials played a leading role in defending the still-foreign ruling dynasty against rebels and western barbarians alike. For their part, the European powers had little sympathy with the

eccentric Taiping form of Christianity, and, having extorted satisfactory agreements from the Qing, they had nothing to gain from the overthrow of the dynasty. An unofficial western mercenary force, 'the Ever-Victorious Army', was assembled to fight the Taiping, commanded in turn by an American, Frederick West, and the British soldier General 'Chinese' Gordon (later famous as Gordon of Khartoum, where he was slain by the forces of another rebel-messiah, the Mahdi). Chinese armies and militias, assisted by the mercenaries, gradually drove back the Taiping, and in 1864 Nanjing itself was stormed; Hong committed suicide and 100,000 of the rebels are said to have fought to the death.

Millions perished during the Taiping revolt, and large areas of China were devastated. Fortunately for the Qing, the Taiping never

Honouring the flag. A Chinese fort destroyed by an Anglo-French punitive expedition. The Arrow War of 1858–60 broke out after a British flag was torn during a Chinese police action.

Top: a government victory against the Taiping rebels, celebrated in a contemporary Chinese painting. During the 1850s there were few such victories, and the rebellion was extinguished only in 1864.

Above: 19th-century painting of the Western 'factories' at Canton from which trade with China was conducted. They became effectively independent enclaves where the imperial writ did not run.

co-ordinated their campaigns with those of two other important insurgent groups. Peasant rebels, the Nian, fought the government for most of the 1860s and 1870s. And ethnic and religious grievances led China's Muslims to rise in the southwest (1855–73) and far to the north in Shaanxi and Gansu (1862–75).

Somehow the dynasty survived, despite the fact that foreign powers continued to humiliate China and extract new concessions. In the 1850s Russia seized vast territories north of the Amur, violating the treaties agreed with Kangxi. Disputes with the British and French led to further hostilities and new treaties; although the powers often acted in a high-handed fashion, the Chinese were also at fault in failing to grasp nuances of western diplomacy (for example, that it was not really acceptable to execute the negotiators despatched by the other side). Hostilities ended in October 1860 after an Anglo-French march on Beijing and the burning of the emperor's summer palace; the Forbidden City itself was spared, probably because it was not in the interest of the powers to destroy the dynasty.

By this time the Qing had begun to understand what they were up against, and some Chinese thinkers were already advocating a cultural compromise: the essential Confucian values would be maintained, but western knowledge ought to be acquired for practical purposes. As part of a 'Self-Strengthening Movement', the study of languages and western-developed sciences was encouraged, and shipyards and arsenals were constructed with the assistance of foreign experts. Previously, several different government departments had dealt with foreigners, but in 1861 a foreign ministry, the Zongli Yamen, was set up – although the court was still unrealistic enough to house it inappropriately, emphasizing its provisional character. Within a few years, however, the court would no longer try to insist that foreign representatives perform the kowtow, and would send abroad ambassadors of its own. Banks, railways and mines, foreign investments, newspapers, missionary schools and publications and students sent abroad all contributed to 'self-strengthening' during the later 19th century.

Unfortunately, every time that some degree of self-strengthing was achieved, new setbacks occurred. The Japanese, closed against the world until the 1850s, had modernized so rapidly after the 1868 Meiji restoration that they were able to join the western powers in taking advantage of China's weakness; as early as 1879 they annexed the Ryukyu Islands, formerly a Chinese tributary. During a brief war in 1884, French forces sank part of China's newly acquired fleet and ended Chinese opposition to colonial expansion in the former tributary territories of South-East Asia. More 'treaty ports' were opened to the powers. And then, in 1894–5, China went to war with Japan. The conflict was triggered by events in Korea, and in effect represented a Japanese challenge to China's long-established suzerainty over the peninsula. Crushing Japanese victories, culminating in the destruction of the Chinese fleet, revealed the success of Japan's modernization and the relative failure (or – much the same thing – sluggishness) of China's programme.

Sun Yatsen (1866–1925), from the 1890s leader-in-exile of the revolutionary republican movement. Chinese of varied political views came to regard him as the father of modern China.

Japan's terms for peace were harsh. The Treaty of Shimonoseki (1895) left Japan as the paramount power in Korea. China ceded Taiwan and the Pescadores, and was only saved from ceding the Liaotung peninsula by the intervention of the European powers, who decided to put a brake on Japanese ambitions. The Chinese paid a huge indemnity and agreed to allow the Japanese to manufacture goods within China itself.

This humiliating defeat led to new calls for change, more radical than the self-strengthening movement. Abroad, a still-unknown Sun Yatsen was creating a revolutionary movement among overseas Chinese, aiming to set up cells inside the country and ultimately replace the Manchu with a republic. But a more immediately influential development was the memorializing of the empire by students assembled in Beijing for the highest (jinshi) examinations. Members of China's future elite, headed by Kang Youwei, advocated a thoroughgoing programme of institutional, industrial

and military development. The urgency of the situation was highlighted by a new scramble for concessions by the foreign states, which were competing against one another with increasing intensity. Areas of China were turning into 'spheres of influence', earmarked for exploitation by a particular colonial power, and it began to seem possible that the process would end in the dismemberment of the country.

China appeared to have found its saviour in the Emperor Guangxu (1875–1908), a young man who was just beginning to exercise real authority after a prolonged regency. In 1898, with the reformer Kang Youwei as his chief adviser, the emperor issued a series of decrees designed to transform education, manufactures and the civil and military government service. The decrees alarmed traditionalists and threatened entrenched interests, which supported a palace coup by the former regent, Cixi. The decrees were cancelled, six leading reformers were executed, and the emperor became a prisoner, secluded in the Forbidden City. Kang Youwei was lucky enough to be on a mission abroad at the time of the coup. He remained in exile, where he was joined by other reformers who managed to avoid

capture, and formed an opposition movement, more moderate than Sun Yatsen's republicans.

Having put an end to 'the Hundred Days' Reforms' and resumed control, the Empress Dowager Cixi wielded power right down to her death in 1908. As a young woman she had become an imperial concubine and had achieved prominence by bearing Xianfeng a son. But when the emperor died in 1861, Cixi became co-regent for the six-year-old Tongzhi and skilfully built up a following at court that consolidated her position. On the death of the childless Tongzhi in 1875, the Empress Dowager was able to secure the throne for her four-year-old nephew Guangxu and a long further lease on power for herself. As the 1898 coup demonstrated, the Empress Dowager's will remained supreme at court even when Guangxu apparently took over, and her subsequent history suggests that she never seriously intended to retire. In the event, Cixi ruled China for over half a century during a critical period in the country's history. For all her political talents, her narrow view of the world and squandermania were China's misfortune, deferring changes that might have strengthened the empire and even saved the dynasty.

Above: when made for the Western market, Chinese porcelain was decorated with subjects of which Chinese artists had little or no experience. On this 18th-century piece the scene is a whale hunt.

Opposite: roundel on the front of a Blue Dragon robe, one of the official costumes of the imperial family and its high officials; embroidered silk. The dragon was the supreme imperial symbol.

END OF AN EMPIRE

Of course Cixi was not an isolated figure on the Chinese scene: her attachment to traditional ways and hatred of the intrusive foreigner was widely shared. Many Chinese were aware of the repeated humiliations inflicted by the powers, but there were also more immediate causes for resentment. Christian missionaries often had a genuine interest in Chinese culture as well as doing valuable medical and educational work. But not all of them were sensitive in their dealings with the Chinese, and the missionaries and their converts occupied a privileged position thanks to the tacit support of the foreign states and their armed forces; in courts of law, for example, Chinese Christians, backed by the missionaries, enjoyed a distinct advantage over their adversaries. Widespread discontent usually had a more directly material cause, but the anger of hungry and exploited peasants was easily directed towards the foreigners and their dupes. This seems to have been the case with the famous Boxer Rising of 1900. Beginning in the Shantung Province on the Yellow River plain, the rising was a spontaneous popular movement that spread across North China without any charismatic leaders emerging from its ranks. Its members combined popular religious practices with the martial arts elements that gave the movement its names, 'Harmony Fists' or 'Boxers United in Righteousness'. Like many earlier Chinese secret societies, the Boxers, short of conventional weapons, practiced austerities and achieved an exalted state of mind in which they believed that weapons could not harm them. Though sadly

Captured Boxers awaiting judgement. The Boxer Rebellion of 1900 represented an enormous but hopeless eruption of popular resentment, directed against foreign domination of China.

inaccurate, such beliefs provided the impetus for resolute, audacious mass action.

By June 1900 large numbers of Boxers had reached Beijing, preceded by news of bloody massacres of missionaries and converts. When the foreign legations in the capital came under threat, Cixi was faced with a difficult decision. The Boxers' slogan was 'Support the Qing, destroy the foreign!' By comparison with the oppressors from overseas, the dynasty evidently felt like a national institution, although in other circumstances the Chinese and Manchus were as conscious as ever of their differences. Constantly faced by new foreign demands, could Cixi risk alienating a huge and apparently irresistible popular movement? She decided that the only way to preserve the dynasty was to ally with the Boxers. Once more underestimating the strength and resources of the foreigners, she declared war on them, and Boxer attacks on the legations turned into a siege that lasted for eight weeks before a mixed-nationality relief force drove off the besiegers and sacked Beijing. The Empress Dowager and Guangxu fled, but the powers again decided that it would not be in their interest to destroy the Qing. However, China was condemned to pay a huge indemnity, and new concessions were imposed, including the fortification of the concessions.

Cixi and the emperor returned to the capital, but the prestige of the dynasty was now in ruins, and even the Empress Dowager recognized the need for change. She strove to conciliate the powers, but the Russo-Japanese war of 1904–5 only emphasized Chinese impotence. Russia, which had advanced into Manchuria with impunity, was defeated by an Asian power far smaller than China, after the belligerents had fought against each other on territory which the Manchus regarded as their own.

Late in the day, serious reforms were mooted. The traditional examinations were abolished in 1905. Long-range plans for constitutional government were announced the following year. The Empress Dowager died in November 1908, followed a day later by Guangxu, still a palace prisoner; the new emperor, Puyu, was an infant who took no part in what followed. Pressure from the newly formed provisional assemblies led to the

meeting of a national assembly in 1910. Attitudes changed with astonishing rapidity, and in the cities pigtails were removed and western dress became common. Despite Manchu concessions, events moved too fast for them to control. An army mutiny in Wuhan sparked a series of mutinies and risings which revealed the strength of anti-Manchu feeling and led to Puyu's abdication in February 1912. But this time not only the dynasty but the long record of the Celestial Empire had come to an end. China entered a new phase in its history, no less turbulent than anything that had gone before.

Puyu, the last Chinese emperor. He abdicated as a child, later became puppet emperor of Japanese-controlled Manchukuo (Manchuria), and died a 'rehabilitated' citizen of Communist China.

2 A WAY OF LIFE

SOCIETY IN IMPERIAL CHINA WAS BASED ON GROUPS IN WHICH HIERARCHY, DEFERENCE AND OBEDIENCE WERE THE RULE. THE IDEA OF INDIVIDUALS AS SEPARATE ENTITIES WITH PERSONAL RIGHTS WAS UNKNOWN: THE INDIVIDUAL HAD MEANING ONLY AS A MEMBER OF A NETWORK OF RELATIONSHIPS, IN WHICH HE (USUALLY HE RATHER THAN SHE) EXERCISED AUTHORITY OVER HIS INFERIORS AND DISPLAYED RESPECT AND OBEDIENCE TOWARDS HIS SUPERIORS. THE SAME PRINCIPLES APPLIED WHETHER THE NETWORK CONSISTED OF A SINGLE HOUSEHOLD, A CLAN, A GREAT ESTATE, OR THE ENTIRE CELESTIAL EMPIRE. IN THEORY, EACH PERSON HAD A KNOWN PLACE IN THE SOCIAL ORDER AND BELONGED TO A GROUP THAT WAS HELD RESPONSIBLE FOR HIS, OR HER, BEHAVIOUR.

superiors than vice versa. The hierarchical principle was extended to the wider (same-surname) family or clan, and to the spirit world in the form of the ancestors who were worshipped at an altar in the house or, by the wealthy, in a separate hall.

FAMILY AND HOUSEHOLD

For those charged with governing a vast empire, treating the population in terms of definable groups and associations made it much easier to maintain order. And from the individual's point of view there was everything to be said for belonging to a group or groups based on mutual assistance. Those who were alone in the world gladly joined an extended family by adoption or as servants, or at least sought the protection of a fraternity, whether it was a guild of craftsmen (including thieves) or a secret society.

The basic social unit was the family, which in its ideal form consisted of three or even four generations of relatives living under the same roof. In the household, the older had authority over the younger, the male over the female, the master or mistress over the servant. These customary relationship were endorsed by Chinese law, which pointedly imposed more severe punishments on inferiors who committed crimes against their

Although family tyrants certainly existed, in theory relationships between superior and inferior involved mutual obligations, the part of the superior being to help, advise and protect the inferior; and this was the model for behaviour throughout society, in which individuals sought to enhance their prospects by ingratiating themselves and their kin with useful patrons, or by building up followings of dependants who would display their authority and back them up in a crisis.

One of the most effective ways of increasing a family's influence was through marriage. In respectable society, marriages were always arranged, and even most peasant families controlled their children's choices with a view to material or other advantages. Wealth was attractive in a prosperous bridegroom, but scholarly achievement (carrying the promise of official eminence) was so highly regarded that it was not unknown for an outstanding examinee to be 'kidnapped' by a wealthy family and persuaded to betroth one of its offspring. In a more conventional negotiation a girl's dowry was an important consideration, but prospective in-laws might be influenced by her reputation for filial piety, since they would have to live with her and might depend on her care in their old age. When a girl

Above: in this delightful ink drawing, a concubine is on her way to join her new master. The presence of one or more concubines in a wealthy household was an accepted situation.

Opposite: a marriage ceremony in Qing China. As in most traditional societies, marriages were arranged by the families of the bride and groom, who were given little or no choice in the matter.

Ladies at their leisure in a garden: a 19th-century view of the Chinese woman as an exemplar of gracious living. The picture is an unusual combination of watercolours and hair embroidery.

married, she took her husband's name, moved into his (or his family's) house, and was expected to behave as a daughter/wife in her new home and effectively forget her own parents and relations. Given such demands, it was vital to secure a dutiful girl who would remain attached to her second family even if her husband died before his parents; Chinese writers were fond of describing heroic widows who refused all marriage offers in order to care for aged in-laws, but it is difficult to be sure whether 'faithful widows' were being heroic or responding to social pressures; the fact that statistical records of such widows were kept, and that their numbers rose steeply during the morally conservative Qing period, is susceptible to more than one interpretation. Since they were important social cults, betrothal and marriage involved

a long sequence of ceremonies and exchanges of cards and presents. Female go-betweens smoothed the arrangements and carried out checks on the suitability of bride and groom by consulting soothsayers. Their prognostications were based on the hour and day of birth of the couple and, if unfavourable, were sufficient to break off the match; if it went ahead, the soothsayer was called in again to fix an auspicious day for the ceremony.

Initially, at least, couples hoped for a boy child. Only a male would be able to perpetuate the family name and perform the necessary ceremonies and sacrifices when his parents joined the ancestors; by contrast, a girl would eventually change her name and become part of a stranger's household. Fertility was so important that sterility was one of the main grounds on which a man might divorce his wife; interestingly, most of the others involved failures of obedience or respect on the part of the wife towards in-laws, provisions that emphasize the collective nature of marriage agreements.

However, it was also possible for a woman to be too fertile. Even in a moderately well-to-do family, the custom of dividing estates between all the male children could lead to a ruinous fragmentation if there were too many sharers; and the poor of both town and country had more pressing reasons to keep down the number of mouths that needed feeding. Consequently infanticide was widely practised (usually by drowning) and thousands of children were abandoned. By the Song era there were so many cases in the cities that foundling hospitals were established and adoption was encouraged.

There seems to be a good deal of justification for the western view of the Chinese in traditional society as a rather cool, self-controlled and polite people, even quite far down the social scale, and it has been suggested that such characteristics had to be developed if several generations were to live together in a single household. There could certainly be internal tensions, especially in upper-class households where the womenfolk led a very enclosed existence, hardly appearing in public; if their number included one or more concubines, the atmosphere could become poisonous, as much

Chinese fiction demonstrates. (A man was perfectly entitled to take a concubine in addition to his wife, although only a small minority of the very wealthy could afford to maintain one.)

Any domestic dramas that occurred were played out against the rather austere background of the Chinese interior. This was essentially a rectangular space divided into rooms by painted or plastered screens. For centuries the occupants sat cross-legged on mats, rugs or cushions, and the general appearance of the interior resembled the traditional type still to be seen in Japan. But during the Tang period the spatial balance was altered when chairs were introduced, tall enough for the occupant to sit upright with feet resting on the ground. Among the few other items of furniture were low tables and beds of matting or, in the cold north, a kang; this very useful object was a platform-sofa-bed of hollowed bricks, heated by flues carrying warm air from an oven. Hanging scrolls were the most popular form of interior decoration, but during later dynasties (from the Song onwards) the growth of antiquarian enthusiasm led connoisseurs to deck rooms with ancient objets d'art. The houses of the affluent might consist of several rectangular structures, arranged so that they surrounded a courtyard. Large gardens, often landscaped to resemble mountains and similar features in miniature, were sources of great pleasure, attached to many houses even in crowded big cities.

Below, left: an elegant but useful household object that still looks serviceable after more than 2,000 years. This bronze lamp dates from the late Zhou period (5th to 3rd century BC).

Below, right: an ordinary family taking a meal together. The photograph dates from the 1890s, but despite the hand-tinting and fixed poses, the people are authentic types.

CHINESE WOMEN

Making music at a banquet: ladies of the Tang imperial court dine together and harmonize on a variety of instruments. This sophisticated but surprisingly informal scene was painted in the 10th century.

As in most pre-modern societies, Chinese women were subordinate to their menfolk in theory and (almost always) in practice. A girl was obliged to obey her father until she married, when she passed under the control of her husband; if she outlived him, she had to submit to the authority of her son. Male supremacy was justified by an appeal to

(among other things) the complementary principles of yin and yang that permeated the universe: men embodied the yang principles of strength, hardness, mastery; women were designed to be yin – weak, yielding and compliant. The female child was more likely to be quietly done away with at birth when it was becoming difficult to feed the entire family, and more likely to be undernourished if there was not enough to go round. A girl received little or no formal education, could not own property, and had her marriage arranged for her. As a new wife she was usually at the beck and call of her in-laws, and if the household was an upper-class one, propriety dictated that she should spend most of her time indoors, embroidering and gossiping, protected from inappropriate contacts, while accepting the presence of her husband's concubines; for their part, the concubines might enjoy a brief favour but were condemned to an inferior status. Security, and perhaps affection, was acquired by producing a male heir.

As always, there were exceptional or lucky women who found wider scope for their talents. The autocratic nature of imperial rule made it inevitable that some emperors should be influenced or manipulated by their womenfolk, although the enclosed, personalized nature of harem politics did not encourage the best qualities in their occupants. Supreme power was only available to a woman who was also the mother of a child-emperor; given such an opportunity, an able schemer such as the Han dowager Lu, the Tang Sovereign Empress Wu and the 19th-century Empress Dowager Cixi could seize power, wield it in public from behind a screen, and hold on to it even when the death of the imperial infant removed the legitimate basis of her authority. In slightly less exalted households a woman of strong personality probably exercised more influence than she was supposed to, but she remained hemmed in by tradition unless she lived long enough to become a revered matriarch and the sole representative of her generation in the family.

Educational barriers kept women from participating in the scholarly and literary culture so central to upper-class Chinese life, but again there were a few exceptions. Ban Zhao (48–117) wrote an exposition of the proprieties, *Lessons for Women*, and was sufficiently learned to complete the history of the Former Han left unfinished at the death of her historian brother, Ban Gu. And the Song period produced one important woman poet, Li Qingzhao (1081–1140), whose happy marriage suggests that legal and customary

restraints did not always blight private life. She married Zhao Mingzheng, a passionate antiquarian whose interests she shared, spending delightful evenings with him scrutinizing old books, paintings and bronzes. But their comfortable life ended when Kaifeng fell to the Jin and they were forced to flee south. Zhao, as an official, was given a dangerous assignment and felt obliged to leave Li behind. When he was taken ill and died, Li set about the pious task of publishing his masterwork, an exhaustive collection of ancient inscriptions on stones and bronzes; and it was in her postscript to the book that she left a touching description of their life together. After her task was accomplished, we hear no more of her.

The talents of girls trained to sing and perform on musical instruments were much appreciated, but their profession was invariably linked with prostitution; in fact brothels were known as 'singing-girl houses'. Theatrical troupes, male and female, were also regarded as part of the profession, whose members ranged from 'flowers' who haunted the city streets, to courtesans so irresistible that respectable men ruined themselves to win their favours. In portraying courtesans, Chinese literature could be as sentimental as its western counterparts. In one story, 'The Whore

A woman at work embroidering; from a European engraving dated 1800. China's patriarchal society offered few opportunities for women to earn money, but the elaborate embroideries of upper-class garments and hangings created a demand for skilled workers.

Above: early photograph of a Chinese girl being dressed on her wedding day. Typical of Chinese fashion, her robe is made of richly decorated material, but is not shaped to her figure.

Opposite: woman with unnaturally tiny feet. For centuries the Chinese sacrificed health to fashion, binding their girl children's feet so tightly that they became deformed.

spin textiles, brew, make preserves, cook and look after the house. Apart from domestic service and prostitution, only a few independent careers were open to women, notably nursing and midwifery; in fact the career situation was not unlike that of 19th-century Europe, except that Chinese women were also able to earn money by acting as go-betweens, arranging marriages at different social levels. A good deal of practical independence was also enjoyed by the wives of shopkeepers and small merchants, who often helped to run the family business.

From an outside point of view, the most bizarre feature of women's lives was foot-binding. This extraordinary practice seems to have started at the Song court and to have become the norm by the 14th century, if not earlier. Little girls' feet were bound tightly with cloth so that the toes were bent under the sole; over years of painful growth, the arch of the foot was broken and the member was hideously deformed; but the object was achieved – to possess what appeared (when concealed by shoes) to be exquisitely tiny feet. Women who had endured foot-binding could only stump about on their heels and were quickly exhausted by walking or standing; nevertheless this upper-class fashion spread through the Han population, defying Manchu efforts to suppress it, and was widely adopted by groups such as farmers' wives and servants, turning already arduous ways of life into tortures. Since foot-binding remained a perfectly normal custom right down to the end of the imperial epoch in 1912, it is unsurpassed as an example of an irrationally destructive fashion which acquires the authority of social custom.

with a Pure Heart', the dissolute emperor Huizong develops an obsessive love for the courtesan Li Shishi; he neglects his duties while hostile Jurchens mass on the borders of his empire, and when they invade it is the courtesan who sacrifices her fortune to help the state and takes her own life rather than become the mistress of a barbarian sovereign. 'The Scholar and the Courtesan' also has western parallels, featuring a heroine who is trapped by circumstances, becomes a brilliantly witty and literate ornament to her profession, but finally succeeds in her ambition to become a respectable wife and mother.

For the majority of girls, education consisted of instruction in traditional domestic and household skills. The country wife or servant girl might have to prepare hemp and look after silkworms,

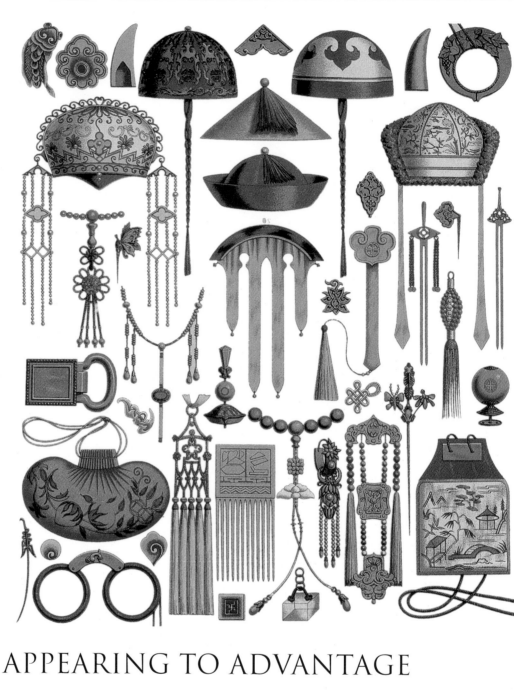

Like a catalogue page of Chinese ornament, this illustration brings together jewellery, spectacles, hats, talismans and a range of other personal accessories used by the Manchu upper class during the late Qing era.

APPEARING TO ADVANTAGE

The Chinese wore clothes for the sake of decency and warmth, but also to display their wealth and rank. Naturally this was of little concern to the poor, who were dressed in hempen blouses and trousers, often tucked up out of the way when they were working. The better-off wore garments of silk, satin, velvet and, in later imperial times, cotton; and where appropriate these were decorated with splendid woven patterns or embroidery. Over the centuries the emperors issued sumptuary decrees defining what might or might not be worn by the different classes (especially the

wealthy but despised merchant class), but prohibitions had a limited effect when confronted by the impulse towards self-assertion and the demands of fashion. Style guides were consulted by would-be dandies, and the cyclical nature of fashion was noted by the 18th-century poet Yuan Mei, who observed that the hat and robe he had worn in his youth had, thirty years later, come back into vogue.

The most explicit documents and the majority of surviving textiles date from the final, Qing dynasty (1644–1912), and the description that follows is largely taken from what is known of this period. Fashion was mainly based on the colours being worn and on details such as the height of a hem-line. The basic garments hardly changed, since there was never any question of shifting the emphasis from one part of the human figure to another. In fact the human outline was not an important feature, and both men and women had no compunction about wearing many layers of clothes; this was most marked in cold weather, since resort was made to the multiplication of 'indoor' clothes rather than to specialized outdoor garments. Men of any standing wore long T-shaped robes with short jackets over them; the jackets might be sleeveless, like waistcoats. Women dressed in somewhat shorter robes above skirts; jackets, also often sleeveless, were worn over the robes, and trousers under the skirts.

The grandest costumes, originally restricted to court circles, were 'dragon robes' of richly embroidered silk, carrying designs of mountains, streams and dragons. A garment worn over the ankle-length dragon robe bore a large panel on the chest and back with devices indicating the official grade of the wearer; by Qing times it was a little shorter than the ankle-length dragon robe, allowing its distinctive wave-patterned hem to be seen. There were also superbly decorated court robes for women, whose use appears to have been more strictly confined to its intended milieu.

The mandarin who dressed in dragon robes also wore a hat crowned by a knob of glass, semi-precious stones or metal which put his official status beyond doubt. There were several types of hat for men, including straw and bamboo models for summer wear. Women occasionally wore scarves, but more often displayed carefully coiffured hair decorated with combs, hairpins and ornaments that were sometimes highly elaborate and burdensomely heavy. Earrings and other jewels were worn by those who could afford them, along with cosmetics that created a doll-like appearance at some danger to health. White lead was a prime ingredient, as it was in Elizabethan England, and had the same effect, which was to ruin the complexion it con-

cealed. Rouge was applied to the whitened face, the eyebrows were plucked and pencilled, lipstick was applied to emphasize (or counterfeit) a small, round mouth, and the fingernails were painted red. Both men and women allowed the nails of their little fingers to grow very long, flaunting

the fact that they were not obliged to perform manual work; once established as a mark of status, the vulnerable nail required protection, a function performed by intricately decorated sheaths of gold and silver. Male ornaments were restricted to hand rings and buckles and plaques worn on belts. Both sexes carried fans and, since pockets were unknown, used the wide sleeves of their garments as substitutes.

Above: a pair of enamelled silver earrings; Qing period, late 18th or early 19th century. Fine ladies wore elaborate and often heavy earrings and hair ornaments, emphasizing the doll-like look created by their white makeup.

Nail protectors worn by the Empress Dowager Cixi, ruler of China until 1908. Excessively long fingernails were fragile status symbols, proving their possessor did no strenuous work.

Right: workers building a dyke; from a scroll painting showing the Emperor Kangxi inspecting their efforts. The threat of floods and the blessings of irrigation have remained constants over 4,000 years of Chinese history.

Below: ploughing the soil. This relief design appears on a brick from a Han tomb and shows an ox drawing the plough. Advanced agricultural techniques enabled the Chinese to sustain a huge population.

ON THE LAND

As in all pre-industrialized civilizations, the entire superstructure of Chinese government and culture owed its existence to the food surpluses produced by the peasantry. Labour on the land nourished the court and the citizens of the great cities. When rural life was disrupted by political and natural disasters, millions perished; but in the long run the population rose ever higher (it was past the hundred-million mark by the Song period, probably reaching a staggering four hundred million by 1850), sustained by the fertility of the land and frequent improvements in farming methods over the centuries.

From the iron ploughshares manufactured in Han state workshops to the quick-growing strains of rice first introduced from Cambodia by the Song, the state played an active role in encouraging agriculture. Officials toured the villages, instructing the inhabitants in the use of new pedal-pump machines for irrigation. State granaries distributed their contents free during harvest failures, and protracted though often ineffective efforts were made to prevent landlords from exploiting tenant farmers. In so far as the state protected the peasant, it did so for its own purposes, since it expected to tax him, make him perform military duties, and employ his obligatory labour on government projects (the corvée) which might or might not be for his personal benefit. At the same time, sensible ministers and offi-

cials realized that it was not in the interests of the empire to drive rural populations so hard that they broke out in revolt.

Despite these state activities, rural communities were too numerous to be constantly supervised and for most of the time they were left to run their own affairs provided they gave no trouble. For their part, villagers had little inclination to become entangled with officialdom and the inflexibility of the law, so there were strong reasons for settling disputes by local arbitration and even administering criminal justice through collective decisions.

Unlike the official, the landlord's agent and the canny lender were always close to hand. The history of rural areas is a blank for long periods in which prosperity and contentment may well have reigned; inevitably, there are much fuller records of personal and general hard times, whether they take the form of bond-servant agreements or histories of peasant uprisings. Such records leave an impression that life was always precarious for lesser folk such as small farmers, tenants and agricultural labourers. Floods or droughts, wars or famines, a bad harvest or bad luck, plunged them into debt, from which very high rates of interest made it difficult ever to escape. A child might have to be sold into service or, if matters became sufficiently desperate, a debtor was faced with the ultimate choice between committing suicide and taking up a new profession as a bandit. If there were enough debtors and bandits, individual misfortune might be transformed into a full-scale uprising, sometimes with fatal consequences for the dynasty.

In normal times, life was evidently endurable, if hard and monotonous. This is possibly the only useful generalization that can be made about a country so regionally diverse and with such a long history as China's. Cereals and rice, vegetables and fruit, meat and fish, tea, opium, silk and timber were all products of the countryside, but by Song times the cereals produced by the rich northern loess had dwindled in importance by comparison with the huge yields of rice from the Yangtze valley and other areas of the South. It was this that brought men and buffaloes to labour from dawn to dusk in vast patchwork vistas of waterlogged fields, cultivating the staple that would be heaped up in canal boats and sent all over the empire. In imperial China, rice, and the peasant who grew it, sustained the sum of things.

Pottery model of a sheep pen; from a tomb of the Han period (202 BC–AD 220). Under the Han, sheep were raised for mutton and sheepskins were used for clothing, but wool was not yet removed from the hide and spun and woven as a textile.

GREAT CITIES

The majority of Chinese have always lived in rural areas. But the size of the population and the development of social hierarchies and sophisticated administrative structures led at an early date to the growth of large and populous cities. In fact, over the past 2,000 years the largest city in the world at any particular time has more often than not been Chinese.

Walled rectangular defensive enclosures appeared in North China as early as the 3rd millennium BC. Extensive remains at Erlitou, in the Yellow River valley, date from about 2000 BC and may well represent one of the capitals of the Xia, China's shadowy first dynasty. This has many features in common with Zhengzhou and Anyang, capitals of the subsequent Shang dynasty (c. 1750–1027 BC) and a number of sites beyond the North China Plain. Xia and Shang cities were formidably walled, using the rammed earth that served the Chinese so well as a concrete-substitute until quite recent times. The important buildings stood on rammed-earth platforms and were thatched and timber-framed, with wattle and daub (clay and twig) infilling. The cities seem to have housed royal or noble elites, serving as defensive and ritual centres; farmers, artisans and other commoners lived at a distance, presumably supplying the elite with commodities and services.

Right: busy street life, possibly as observed at Kaifeng, the Song capital, around 1100; detail from a much larger work on a scroll, 'Along the River at the time of the Qingming Festival,' painted by Zhang Zeduan.

Below: the gardens of the emperor's Summer Palace in Beijing, with its celebrated marble bridge. Such imperial gardens were really vast parks, enclosing varied landscape features, pavilions and so on.

Above: Chinese street scene. The picture is obviously a Western production, emphasizing oriental 'quaintness' (down to the inclusion of a pagoda in the far distance), but it nevertheless captures the teeming life of the city.

Opposite: the marble boat in the gardens of the Summer Palace at Beijing. A splendid folly (but a folly all the same), it was made for the Empress Dowager Cixi, who diverted sorely needed money from the naval budget to pay for it.

Arguably such exclusive areas should be regarded as ceremonial centres rather than true cities, which only developed during the Eastern Zhou period (770–221 BC). These were walled and featured platformed palaces, but they also contained large residential areas and functioned as centres of trade and manufacturing, especially of iron implements. After the triumph of the north-western state of Qin and the foundation of the empire, Xianyang became the capital, and the site (modern Xi'an) proved so convenient that it was more than once sacked, destroyed and rebuilt nearby. As Changan, just across the River Wei from Xianyang, it served as the imperial capital under the Former Han and Tang dynasties, with Luoyang in the north-east (also several times rebuilt) as its twin or alternative capital.

With its million-strong population and 36-kilometre-long walls, Tang Changan was certainly the greatest city in the world. It was also one of the most cosmopolitan, functioning as the eastern terminus of the trade routes across Central Asia and welcoming diplomats, merchants, missionaries and refugees from many lands. Yet, like all Chinese cities built under the early imperial dynasties, Changan was carefully planned and, in intention, subject to strict control. Its gates were oriented to the points of the compass and it was built on a grid plan as strict as present-day New

York's. A magnificent broad avenue led straight from the southern gate to a huge (but not the sole) imperial palace. Temples and markets stood at designated locations. The palace and administrative areas were sealed off from the residential quarters, which were divided into 108 walled compounds or wards which were locked up every night. Though close supervision of the city population was physically impossible, the Tang, like their Han predecessors who occupied a nearby site, strove to ensure that any trouble could be localized and prevented from threatening the security of the state.

By the Song era, big cities were no longer rigidly planned, but grew – or sprawled – in more organic fashion. The Northern Song capital, Kaifeng, had become an important metropolis even earlier, during the Five Dynasties period. It was conveniently sited, lying just below the Yellow River, close to its junction with the Grand Canal along which barges brought vast quantities of rice from the South to feed the urban population. But in 1127 North China was overrun by the Jurchens and the surviving (Southern) Song took up residence at Hangzhou. They never publicly accepted that Kaifeng was lost for good, referring to Hangzhou as Xing Cai, 'the Temporary Residence'; the name stuck, and even when the Southern Song had been replaced by the

Mongol Yuan dynasty, the Venetian traveller-merchant Marco Polo was informed that the name of the city was 'Qinsai'.

Hangzhou was the first capital of China to be located outside the North, which was both the historic heartland of the state and, in effect, the command centre from which the activities of the steppe peoples could be monitored. Hangzhou's warmer climate may have been partly responsible for its relaxed atmosphere, but it also reflected the quality of life under the Southern Song. Beautifully situated among mountains, lakes and rivers, the city overflowed its walls as commerce and pleasure promoted population growth. Changan may have been a more lively place than our knowledge of its walled compounds suggests, but there is no doubt at all about Hangzhou. Guidebooks have survived from the Southern Song period that list its amenities, confirming the slightly later account of Marco Polo; he may have been influenced by Hangzhou's network of canals which made it resemble his native Venice, but he was certainly correct in believing that it was the greatest city in the world. Although there were closed-off dwellings such as grand houses with large gardens, there were also terraces opening on to the streets and, as well as official markets, rows of ground-floor shops; most of them sold everyday commodities, but specialists existed to cater for every possible want, from rhinosceros skins to antiques. Tourists, travellers and pleasure-seekers were welcomed at inns, taverns and tea-houses, while the bill of fare at restaurants included regional dishes as well as luxury and local cuisine. Street-vendors and entertainers enlivened the scene and, if Marco Polo is to be believed, the city was thronged with girls whose commercially available charms so enchanted the visitor that, when forced to leave, he longed for the day when he would be able to return. There may have been an element of colourful exaggeration in Polo's effusions (or those of the professional romance-writer Rustichello, who put his memoirs into publishable form), but the fact that he twice describes Hangzhou as 'Paradise' would seem to imply genuinely fond memories. On the other hand it is clear that the city also suffered from familiar metropolitan ills such as proletarian poverty, overcrowding and soaring crime rates. The traditional Chinese city reached its apogee during the Song era, and later centres had few new features until European innovations were introduced in Canton and other 19th-century ports. In terms of still-visible spectacle, Beijing (Peking) is outstanding, quite apart from the role it played in the history of the late empire. The first Yuan emperor, Kublai Khan, made the city his winter capital (spending his summers in Mongolia at Shang Tu, evidently in the hope of counteracting the softening influence of China on his entourage). But it was the Ming emperor Yongle who effectively created the closed imperial world known as the Forbidden City in its present form, with its halls, courtyards and colonnades, pavilions, gardens and marble terraces. This northern inland city was not an entirely logical choice for a Han Chinese emperor, but its position roughly midway between Manchuria and the fertile Yangtze valley made it the preferred residence of the Manchu Qing dynasty, relegating its rival, Nanjing, to a secondary (though important) role. Beijing witnessed the most glorious days of the Qing, the Anglo-French sacking of the Summer Palace, the setting up of a quarter assigned to foreign legations, the Boxer siege, the flight and return of the Empress Dowager, and the abdication of the last emperor, Puyu. The later Manchu sovereigns had been even more cloistered than earlier emperors, hardly ever leaving the Forbidden City, and this remained true of Puyu even after he had given up the throne. Lavishly subsidized and retaining his imperial title, he lived through the chaotic early years of the republic in the Forbidden City, from which he was finally expelled by an ambitious warlord in November 1924. The end of an imperial presence, coinciding with the temporary loss of its status as China's capital, decisively thrust Beijing into the new era.

Opposite: country magistrates taking part in an examination. Provincial and national papers were set to enable candidates to qualify for office at a variety of levels – a concept unknown outside China before the 19th century.

THE ELITE

Among the most unusual features of imperial Chinese society were the elite role played by the scholar-official or mandarin class and the examination system through which so many of its members were selected. Grounded in the Confucian classics, the mandarin was responsible for most aspects of Chinese life that government could hope to control or influence. And he could aspire to the highest positions, as one of the emperor's ministers, since the distinction between civil service and government hardly existed in a land where all were the emperor's servants and advisers.

The prestige of the mandarins was based on their service to the state, but it was all the greater because, after the early Tang period, China lacked a traditional aristocracy to monopolize high office and dominate localities through their land-holdings. Families might become wealthy and powerful, but the Chinese custom of dividing inheritances equally between heirs worked against the establishment of large, enduring estates. Even when service to the state brought wealth, the service had to be renewed, generation after generation, if a family was to maintain its standing. So the scholar-official became a social ideal and, at least from Song times, it was the independently wealthy who sought (or bought) degrees and aped the style of mandarins, and not, as might have been supposed, vice versa.

Selection for official posts on the basis of merit, as ascertained by some kind of examination, can be traced back to the Han era. In 196 BC an imperial decree ordered provincial governors to send suitable candidates to Changan, where their abilities would be assessed, and by the 1st century BC formal examinations were being held annually. Schools were set up to train candidates, but there can never have been much chance of a peasant's son attending; even much later, when some degree of literacy was much more widespread, only a tiny minority would be able to study for the protracted period needed to master the thousands of characters comprising the Chinese script, let alone acquire the intimate knowledge of the Confucian classics on which the examinations came to be based. Nevertheless men from very humble backgrounds did rise through the examination system; this probably means that their intelligence was somehow noticed, leading to their being sponsored by a wealthy individual or recognized institution.

For centuries, officials selected by examination remained a minority, and even when studying to qualify became the norm (under the Song) it was still possible for an official to place his son, as of right, in the service. However, all the most important posts under the Song and subsequent dynasties were restricted to degree-holders, and their prestige was such that no one with a chance of passing an examination would have given up the opportunity to do so. During the 19th century, when the embattled Qing were desperate for funds, degrees were put up for sale and found thousands of purchasers.

Not surprisingly, the examinations were momentous events, deciding the destinies of thousands of young men, and of some older men who attempted them again and again. Candidates worked in rows of individual cubicles, and ingenious methods of cheating were met by equally ingenious counter-measures: at one time the question to be answered by an individual examinee was not known until the last moment, when an arrow was fired at a list pinned up in the cubicle; the question it transfixed was the one the candidate was required to attempt. Successful candidates proceeded from the local to the provincial, and finally to the national examination. Even passing the lowest-level examination brought solid benefits in the form of a small stipend and exemption from corporal punishment and the corvée. There were some career opportunities for those who passed at provincial level, while the national degree-holders had an assured future as members of the mandarin elite. Although it was possible to gain qualifications in mathematics and other specialist subjects, the study of the Confucian classics was the real key to advancement. For a long time, literary and analytical ability was rewarded, and a Tang scholar such as Yuan Zhen could come out first in the examinations by writing an essay critical of imperial policies; but under the despotic Ming, rote learning and strict orthodoxy of interpretation were absolutely insisted upon. The situation remained unchanged until the 19th century, when it became clear that the training of the bureaucracy made them unfit to cope with the new ways being forced upon China. A few reformers hoped to restore genuine Confucian values to the sterile existing system, but the rush to westernize, when it came, proved irresistible. In 1905 the examination system was abolished, and with it the unique mandarin class.

A 19th-century painting of a tea depot. Tea was a major Chinese export, especially in demand from the British – whose consequent balance of payments difficulties made them eager to sell opium to China.

MERCHANTS AND TRADE

For most of Chinese history, merchants were assigned to a low place in the social scale, ranking below officials, farmers and artisans. Trade was looked down on by high-minded Confucians as a non-productive activity which promoted the use of superfluous luxuries. The activities of merchants, with their changing fortunes, were at variance with the ideal of a stable society in which every individual had a fixed place. Moreover, if a merchant became wealthy it was by dealings very different from those associated with the conventional route of state service, and produced a different personality and tastes from those of the scholar-official elite. Like the European bourgeois, the Chinese merchant was for centuries held up to scorn as a vulgar fellow whose manners

and social aspirations were inherently ludicrous. In their preoccupation with stability, the imperial authorities attempted to keep control of the economy, making the production of key commodities (salt, alcohol, coins, gunpowder) state monopolies, fixing prices and, down to the Song period, confining urban commerce to designated market areas. State-run enterprises, even under the easy-going Song, extended to tea-houses on the imperial highways featuring singing-girls, and the pleasure grounds and brothels of Hangzhou were supervised by a scholar-official. In practice the controls were less far-reaching than they seemed; merchants were often able to circumvent them, and on many occasions they were employed as agents by the authorities, who

Road across Central Asia. In Han times, caravans leaving Changan could travel for 1,500 kilometres through Chinese territory before emerging from the shadow of the Great Wall and crossing Central Asia; under the Tang the first part of the journey was even safer, since the oasis city-kingdoms were ruled by the Chinese or acknowledged imperial suzerainty. There were actually northern and southern 'roads' skirting the desert, taken by caravans after consideration of the political situation and depending on whether they were intended for India, Persia or the Levant. However, it was not usual for a single caravan to travel such distances, if only because a knowledge of local conditions was vital to the security of the goods it carried; consequently these passed through several hands before reaching their final destination. Only luxury items could be traded profitably over such vast distances, and so silk (produced by methods unknown outside China) was the major

A 19th-century Chinese watercolour, showing a money-lender weighing and counting his takings. Financial dealings had a long history in imperial China, where moneylenders were as unpopular (and useful) as in other societies.

subcontracted to them such vital undertakings as keeping the frontier garrisons supplied.

Under the early dynasties there were only limited opportunities for individual trading at anything except village level. But in 199 BC an imperial edict implied that merchants were already getting above themselves: they were forbidden to wear silk clothing, to ride on horses (at this date still regarded as aristocratic beasts), or to carry arms. Since laws are not made against non-existent abuses, we can be fairly sure that merchants had been doing all three things.

From Han times, the greatest opportunities lay in foreign trade. Relations with China's nomad neighbours were a mixture of diplomatic gift-giving and genuine exchange; the exact roles played by official and private enterprise are not easily disentangled, but it seems clear that these dealings were one important source of Han merchant prosperity. Another was the celebrated Silk

Above: the manufacture of porcelain, the most prized of ceramics, is celebrated in this scene on wallpaper. The factory is taking a delivery of petuntse, one of the most important ingredients of porcelain.

Opposite: the junk came in various sizes and was an essential carrier for inland, coastal and seaborne trade. Popularly viewed in the West as quaint, it was in fact a technologically very advanced sailing ship.

Chinese export; but spices, ceramics and fine bronze wares were also carried. In the Han era these eventually reached the Levantine provinces of the Roman Empire, and some were transported as far as Rome itself. The Silk Road trade was certainly more important to the West than to China; payment seems to have been almost exclusively in precious metals and stones, with the significant exception of big horses from Ferghana in Central Asia, imported because they were a great improvement, especially from a military point of view, on Chinese ponies.

The Silk Road flourished under the Tang dynasty, and internal trade also grew, largely thanks to the canal system constructed by the Sui emperors. In the later 8th century the expansion of Arab power in Central Asia disrupted traffic along the Silk Road, encouraging the development of seaborne trade. This was initially conducted by foreign merchants, who settled in large numbers in the southern parts of Canton and Yangzhou. But by the Song era, Chinese merchants and Chinese junks predominated on sea routes extending to India and the Persian Gulf.

The status of the merchant improved as commerce became increasingly important inside China. Under the Tang, no merchant's son was allowed to take the state examinations, a prohibition which emphasized the social inferiority of the wealthy trader to the poor farmer or artisan. But towards the end of the dynasty the rules were relaxed, and a spectacular commercial expansion from the 9th century onwards created a much more diverse society and a city culture in which the 'merchant' class expanded, taking in shopkeepers, restaurant owners, bankers and shipbuilders. The wealthiest began to be accepted for most practical purposes as members of the official elite, and an outside observer might have supposed that China was moving towards capitalism.

Such an impression would have been reinforced by the early circulation of paper money, one of many Chinese inventions. The Chinese were also pioneers in the use of coins, first issuing them at about the same time (the 7th century BC) as the Lydians and Greeks in Western Asia. Chinese legend puts the invention back a further 2,000 years, but the earliest known coins, issued by states during the Eastern Zhou period, were cast in bronze and took the form of miniature spades, knives and other implements. These remained in use until the Qin unification of China in the 3rd century BC, when the emperor Shi Huangdi introduced a simple, round coin with a square hole in the middle. This, the cash, remained the standard Chinese coin down to recent times, carried with relative convenience on a string threaded through the hole. Most calculations were based on strings of a hundred cash, but state accounting dealt in thousands or taels.

The expansion of commerce under the Song led to a shortage of coins and the development of paper money from credit instruments such as bills of exchange. The drawbacks as well as the benefits of the new form of money became apparent when the declining dynasty issued too many notes and caused a serious outbreak of inflation. The succeeding Yuan dynasty found an enthusiastic chronicler in Marco Polo, who marvelled at the Great Khan's ability to create a form of wealth (banknotes) 'which costs him nothing', a belief evidently shared by the later Mongol emperors, whose over-issues created another bout of inflation. The conservative-minded Ming, having reintroduced paper money in 1374, decided that it was not to be relied on and began to phase it out after 1450; it was not reintroduced until the 1850s, at a time when China had begun to feel the impact of the West. So the Chinese innovation, although a notable 'first', was not in practice much of a success.

This start-stop-start pattern typified Chinese economic development: however promising it was at times, no take-off occurred that would transform it and lead on to an industrial revolution. Under the Yuan, merchants enjoyed much greater freedom, but state control was reimposed by the Ming. The status of merchants gradually improved, and by the Manchu period the emperor himself was prepared when on tour to accept the hospitality of big-businessmen. But respectability could still be achieved only by subscribing to the scholar-official ideal: the successful merchant passed himself off as a gentlemen by buying land and patronizing literature and the arts, and he had his son educated in the classics and entered for the state examinations in order that he might join the official elite. The imperial attitude towards the non-Chinese world remained patronizing and suspicious, and when western traders appeared they were regarded as tribute-bearing barbarians for whom a bureaucratic niche had to be found. Though individual Chinese merchants were happy to trade covertly with foreigners, the authorities would only allow official intercourse with one merchant association in a single port. The diplomat Lord Macartney returned to Britain with a letter from Qianlong to George III in which the emperor complacently declared, 'We have never valued ingenious articles, nor do we have the slightest need of your country's manufactures.' And so anti-commercialism persisted into the disastrous 19th century, to be reversed only when it was too late in the day to save the imperial regime.

Right: two-wheeled carriage with driver and umbrella; one of several bronze models found in the tomb of a 2nd-century AD official of the Later or Eastern Han. The number of carriages possessed by an official indicated his rank.

TRANSPORT AND TRAVEL

Throughout the history of Imperial China, most people who travelled by land had no alternative but to walk. Horses were domesticated during the 2nd millennium BC, under the Xia or the Shang, but only a minority could afford to acquire and maintain them. Long distances were covered on foot by groups such as conscripts or peasants fleeing pillage or emigrating to settle more fertile land; the majority, at most times, stayed at home.

However, there were many others who were able to make journeys and carry goods in a much more convenient way: by water. Although the Yellow River valley was the birthplace of ancient China, the river itself was liable to flooding and not navigable along its length. But the Yangtze, further south, became China's main artery, and was only the largest of a number of navigable river systems which made it possible to penetrate deep into the country. Movement was facilitated by canal construction from the 5th century BC, and coastal trade also flourished from the same period. Quantities of goods could be carried by rafts or simple, flat-bottomed boats (sampans) whose oarsmen were remarkably skilled at negotiating

difficult or dangerous stretches of a river. Later on it became vital for the northern cities to be fed with rice from the fertile Yangtze valley, and the Grand Canal provided the missing north-south waterway – ultimately extending for some 1,700 kilometres – that linked the mainly east-west river systems. Although sometimes neglected during disorderly or corrupt eras, the Grand Canal retained its importance through all the dynastic periods and right up to the late 20th century.

The unification of China made internal travel easier and safer. An early result was the construction of an imperial road and bridge network which, among other things, served the officials and army units that travelled long distances to and from the provinces. The central lane of the highway was reserved for the emperor's use, but officials rode on the outside on horseback or, much more often, in carriages or coaches. Under the Han, improvements in transport included the invention of the wheelbarrow and the introduction of the donkey from the West through the barbarian Xiongnu; this gave China a useful pack-animal, although the abundance of available

Left: servants carrying sedan chairs. This photograph of c.1875 shows a mode of transport that disappeared in the West after the 18th century. Like the modern limousine, the sedan chair combined pomp with privacy.

and cheap human labour always provided serious competition for it. At about the same time the ox-cart came into wide use as an inexpensive substitute for the horse-drawn carriage. Camels were confined to the north-west, where they served as the indispensable pack-animals for the Silk Road caravans; but finds of camel tomb figures suggest that they had a certain exotic charm in the eyes of the Chinese. City living also gave rise to new forms of transport; in the sedan chair, carried by porters, ladies could move from place to place in seclusion, while the Song capital, Hangzhou, was criss-crossed by canals and so was able to support a fleet of sturdy water-taxis.

The expansion of commerce under the Song led to a dramatic increase in maritime traffic and the construction by the Chinese of big sea-going ships. The technical innovations of the period, combined with the use of the compass, made possible the great voyages of Zheng He under the Ming, before Chinese society started to become fatally inward-looking. The Chinese sailing vessel, the junk, is identifiable by its short, square bow and stern, and by the absence of a keel. It took a number of forms, of which the simplest has been described as 'a floating packing crate', hardly articulated beyond its internal divisions into three watertight compartments – a major Chinese discovery, incidentally, which made it possible for a vessel to stay afloat even after it had been badly holed.

In its most developed form, the ocean-going junk was a masterpiece of design. Its seemingly quaint appearance in fact reflected its severely functional qualities, which included several inno-vative features. It was furnished with a rudder, a device known at least as early as the Han period, a thousand years before western mariners adopted it. Its highly distinctive sails were made of matting braced with sets of bamboo battens; this 'roller-blind' arrangement enabled seamen to furl and unfurl the sails from the deck (instead of climbing up and down the rigging), and also meant that the amount of sail exposed to the wind could be varied according to its strength. Moreover the alignment of the sails (fore-and-aft rigging) overcame a major seafaring problem, allowing the junk to sail into the wind. The largest junks were enormous, capable of housing dozens of cabins, hundreds of passengers or soldiers, and scores of tonnes of heavy goods. As the voyages of Zheng He demonstrated, the Chinese might have become masters of the Indian ocean had they so chosen; and in that case the fate of the Portuguese explorers and later western expeditions might have been very different.

Below: Chinese cargo boats had a surprisingly large storage capacity. Features such as the moveable panels and 'Venetian blind' sail, shown here, were typical of Chinese ingenuity and practical efficiency.

A tense moment during the hunt. The hunters' alertness, the stealth of the trackers and the gesture restraining the dog are all wonderfully captured; 17th-century ink and sepia-wash painting on silk.

LEISURE TIME

Most western images of old China emphasize the part played in its way of life by restraint, refinement and tranquillity of spirit. The Chinese gentleman at leisure is pictured as composing poetry with measured, skilful strokes of his brush pen, or, out of doors in his garden, playing chess and drinking rice wine with his friends while gazing at the moon or distant mountains.

This does correspond to the ideal of the scholar-official class, but most Chinese would have dutifully admired it without being tempted to imitate it. More physically demanding activities had a long history, among the earliest being a martial arts tradition stretching back to the 1st millennium BC. As in many other cultures, hunting ceased to be a practical activity but survived as a sport until the intensive cultivation of land marginalized it; and during the horse-loving Tang era, polo, probably imported from Iran, was

the most popular upper-class pastime. As the Confucian-literati outlook increasingly gave the tone to Chinese society, their distaste for warlike or boisterous pursuits did diminish the popularity of archery and fencing outside military circles; but this did not prevent the Song emperor Taizu from enjoying a game of football, or diminish the popularity of boxing, wrestling, rowing, horse and dog racing, arrow-throwing competitions (a kind of reversed hoop-la, the target being the narrow neck of a vase), and noisy spectator sports such as cock-fighting.

All of these offered opportunities for gambling, a Chinese passion which neither Confucian moralizing nor imperial decrees were able to suppress. Board games too were not necessarily tranquil affairs. The Chinese versions of chess and Go, the most difficult of all mind-games, sometimes occasioned violent disputes and even homicide, while Liu Bo, a dice-and-counter game resembling backgammon, was more widely popular and much-betted-on. In this and other games, the 'dice' might be marked bamboo sticks, gathered and flung down, or cubes essentially the same as the modern form. Wry entertainment must have been provided by games of the snakes-and-ladders type in which the players won favour or met with disgrace, climbing up or abruptly descending the hierarchy of official posts; presumably this was more popular among non-scholars than with the officials who were at risk in the real world. Dominoes, mahjong and playing cards – a Chinese invention – were also engaged in with unConfucian gusto.

Most Chinese worked hard and had little time or energy for leisure pursuits. But the major annual festivals offered enjoyment for all, especially in the teeming, colourful environment of the big city. As with their religious beliefs, the Chinese seem to have been happy to celebrate any kind of festival, whether official or popular, Buddhist or Daoist. The most important was the New Year, which fell somewhere around 1 February; prefaced by sacrifices to the household gods and the ancestors, and by sweeping and washing down doorways, this festival of renewal was celebrated relatively quietly, by putting on fresh clothes and attending family gatherings. The new year and the coming of spring were given a less decorous welcome a week or two later, at the Feast of Lanterns. This was a spectacular affair lasting three days and also three nights, lived through by many revellers in a state of alcoholic exaltation. Every family strove to outdo neighbours in the splendour and ingenuity of its lanterns and decorations, and in the lavishness of its banquets; competition was so intense that some city householders are said to have ruined themselves rather than be bested.

The Festival of the Dead, in April, was preceded by another ritual of renewal, in this instance not unlike one practiced by the Aztecs. All fires were put out for two days; then, outside the imperial palace on the third day, a spark was laboriously struck by boring wood (presumably representing the making of the first fire of all), flames were lit from it, and new fires were started

everywhere. At the Festival of the Dead, ancestral graves were swept clean and offerings made. However, the holiday was also used for outdoor pleasures such as leisurely boating and forms of nature-appreciation which were prominent among Chinese pleasures. Expeditions were made to view beauty-spots famous for their trees, shrubs and flowers, or to scan the night sky at propitious moments. Autumn was a particularly favoured season, and at this time of year kite-flying, always a popular pastime, took on a symbolic

significance; officials in particular hoped that going up to a high place and flying their kites still higher would, by sympathetic magic, enable them to rise in the world.

By the sophisticated Song period, festivals in the cities were marked by shows, sporting competitions and street entertainments. Many of these were to be found even at quieter times, especially in specially set-aside 'pleasure grounds' reminiscent of 18th-century European haunts such as

Shopping during festival time: a leisured gentleman rides along the street, accompanied by burdened servants, while haggling goes on in the shops; a detail from the handscroll by Zhang Zeduan also shown on pages 86-7.

Vauxhall Gardens beside the Thames in London; a further resemblance lies in the relaxation of ceremonial in the interests of informal contacts and enjoyments. The pleasure grounds of the Song capital, Hangzhou, offered sexual provender, music-dramas, marionette shows, performances by professional storytellers, stand-up comedians, jugglers and acrobats, and a variety of other bizarre entertainments including snake-charming and dancing fish. But there were also a num-

drink. As well as tea-houses and taverns, there were high-class restaurants and street-stalls vending instant snacks. Chinese cuisine had already taken essentially the form in which it is known today, including many regional specialities and variations; however, some ingredients from Europe and the Americas, such as sweet potatoes and tomatoes, were only introduced under the Manchus. Based on the ingenuity of generations of frugal peasants, Chinese cooking made maxi-

Shooting at the mark. Archers queue up to compete for the prize, while a drummer gives the signal to fire, or perhaps simply adds a note of drama to the event. In the background, a mounted man shows off his skill.

ber of performing academies in the pleasure grounds, with instructors who gave lessons in singing, playing an instrument and acting, presumably catering to wealthy amateurs of the arts.

By Song times the city also boasted a range of hostelries offering accommodation and food and

mum use of every known ingredient and a range of spices, which added a variety of tastes to consumption of the universal staple, rice; millet and wheat, though still grown in the North, had long since ceased to rival it in importance. Most poor people lived on rice with vegetable side-dishes;

fish and meat, most often pork, were reserved for special occasions; a peculiarity of Chinese agriculture was the absence of dairy farming, except in the far-western provinces, and consequently the non-consumption of milk and cheese.

Food was cut up into small pieces before being served, so that chopsticks could be used for any dish. Chopsticks dated back at least to the Shang period, but the economical stir-fry technique, using a wok, appeared somewhat later and only gradually assumed its current prominence. Meals were taken from small dishes at a low table, and each course was accompanied by a cup of rice wine. Chinese literature makes much of drunkenness, perhaps because it offered an emotional release from the rectitude and restraint imposed by the Confucian ideal; China's most revered poet, Li Bo (701–62), and its premier novelist Cao Xeqin (1715–63), though separated by seven centuries, were both associated with alcoholic excess, and at some festivals it was a point of honour with celebrants not to go home sober. However, there was no Chinese equivalent to whiskey or gin. 'Rice wine' was in fact a kind of ale, distilled into many varieties by skilful spicing and drunk slightly warm. Marco Polo, his desire to astonish overcoming his patriotism, declared that rice wine was superior to wine made from grapes and much preferred by the Chinese, who had known of it since the Tang era; nevertheless some connoisseurs seem to have consumed grape wine, and the Song emperors had their own private stock, made from vines grown in the imperial park. Rice wine's only rival was the universal drink, tea, known from Han times, established as an empire-wide habit under the early Tang, and cultivated in innumerable varieties to suit all tastes and incomes.

Left: Hong Kong Chinese women at tea, combining pleasure with ceremony. The photograph was taken in about the 1880s, by which time tea had been widely drunk in China for well over a thousand years.

Below: a 19th-century record of the Festival of Lanterns. As it suggests, the festival was an excuse for competitive displays in which families strove to outdo one another in the size and ingenuity of their exhibits.

THE MAKING OF BOOKS

The Chinese language was written from at least the 2nd millennium BC, a development that helped to create a unified China and also went far to ensure its cultural supremacy in East Asia, where neighbouring societies belatedly adapted its script to their own tongues. In China itself, the earliest known use of the script was to record the sessions in which Shang kings divined the future through communion with the ancestors. Other cultures have devised writing systems for mundane purposes such as inventory-making, and it has been suggested that its sacred origin under the Shang explains the reverence and aesthetic delight inspired in the Chinese by calligraphy; executed with an ink-loaded brush capable of producing distinct thick and thin strokes, Chinese calligraphy came to rank as an art, interlinked with poetry and painting.

Until quite recent times, reading and writing have everywhere been elite skills. This was true of imperial China, despite the existence of state and private schools designed to foster talent in the interests of civil service recruitment. Moreover the Chinese writing system was exceptionally difficult, since it was not based on a phonetic alphabet. Every symbol or character expressed a single object or idea, and consequently there were a very large number of characters that had to be learned: by the Han period there were about 9,000, a figure that would eventually rise to 60,000. People who did not aspire to be classical scholars needed to known only a tenth of that number, but even such a lesser level of attainment represented a substantial investment of time and energy.

By 221 BC, when Shi Huangdi created the Chinese empire, a written literature existed that included poetry, philosophical and moral discourses, and historical records. The First Emperor's 'Burning of the Books' represented a malign tribute to the power of the written word; quite how much was lost is difficult to say, but clearly the Confucian tradition was not destroyed and the chief minister's totalitarian slogan – 'No one is to use the past to criticize the present' – could not be put into practice with enduring success. Meanwhile standardization of the written language proceeded, and by AD 220 it had effectively taken on its final form.

The emperor and his wealthier subjects could afford to have their reading matter copied on to silk sheets, but most early writings existed in a much clumsier form. They were inscribed on

Opposite, top: examples of Chinese script, from a 17th-century text for European use. With tens of thousands of characters to be learned, ability to write was the key to membership of the elite.

Right: a 19th-century water pot in the form of a coiled snake. Among the upper classes, even small utilitarian objects were beautifully made and, typically, took animated forms.

strips of wood or bamboo, each wide enough to accommodate a single column of characters or numbers; the strips were holed or notched so that they could be tied together to create sections of a book or administrative files. Then one of the most momentous of all Chinese inventions appeared: paper, traditionally said to have been made in AD 105 by Cai Lun, who cut the cost of supplying the imperial workshop with silk by pulping and pressing silk rags, mulberry bark, hemp and other fibres. The new material seems to have been adopted only gradually, and in 175 it was still regarded as worthwhile to give truly permanent form to the Confucian classics by engraving them on stone tablets. The project took eight years to complete and did have the advantage of enabling scholars and students from all over China to visit the site and make their own copies – on paper.

By the 4th or 5th century, paper had become the writing material used for all but the most consciously lavish effects. Books were designed as sets of scrolls, the text on each scroll consisting of a single long sheet that was gradually wound out from a wooden roller.

Another great Chinese invention dated from the Tang period. Printing from metal or wooden blocks was probably carried out from the 8th century, although the earliest known printed book is a copy of the Buddhist Diamond Sutra, dated 868. At first serving as a cheap and rather shoddy substitute for hand-written work, printing rapidly improved, and by the 10th century the imperial government was commissioning large, lavish editions of the Confucian classics and the Buddhist canon; over 400,000 copies of the latter survive to emphasize the vast scale on which the Chinese state operated. Shortly afterwards the scroll was replaced by printed sheets sewn together to produce books, or rather booklets of which a number were boxed together to make up a single work.

From 1040 printing was also done with movable type (individually cut characters instead of block printing); but the sheer number of Chinese characters hindered its effectiveness, so that it never achieved the revolutionary impact that it had when introduced in the West four centuries later. The workmanship of block printing was often superb, and while state sponsorship led to the production of literary, medical and encyclopaedic works, commercial operators put out large cheap editions of popular and dialect works. Illustrated books were a particular feature of the Ming period, when colour printing was perfected.

A water-dropper in the form of a mandarin duck. Writing was done with a brush, after water had been dropped on to an ink stone, where it was mixed with dry ink from a cake or stick.

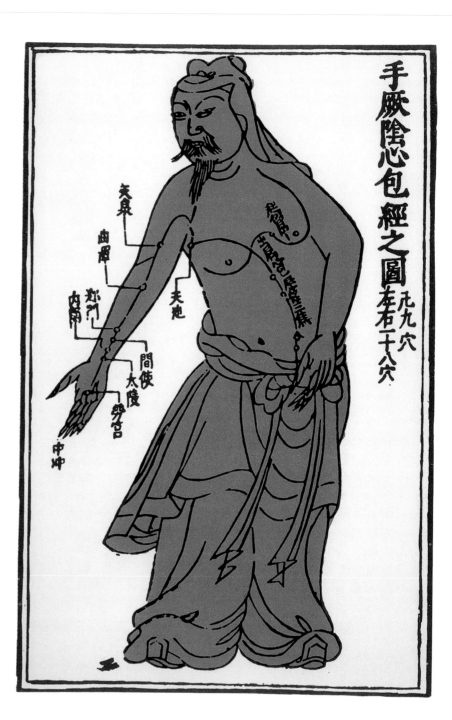

Right: an 11th-century acupuncture chart showing meridians (lines of vital force) and the pressure points along them. In China, acupuncture has been a recognized form of medical treatment for 2,000 years or more.

HEALTH AND MEDICINE

The Chinese approach to health care brought together a number of elements that would now be regarded as incompatible. When taken ill, an individual might blame malign demons, dietary excesses or a failure to keep open the body's energy channels; more to the point, most patients would consult the appropriate practitioners in each area, turning from one to the next when a treatment appeared to have had no result.

Charms, amulets, talismans and ceremonies of exorcism were all in common use by the 1st millennium BC, and arguably remained the most popular form of 'medicine' until the twilight of the imperial era.

The boundary between magic and medicine was also blurred when it came to treatments involving herbs and drugs. Many of these were identified and employed for their curative properties on the basis of observation and experience, but much of the original research was prompted by the quest for an Elixir of Life, associated with Daoist belief and ardently pursued by several emperors. The recipes were often based on the notion that any prescription for immortality must necessarily require high-value ingredients (gold, silver, pearls), which makes it likely that they had the opposite effect to the one desired.

Herbals and pharmacopoeias were in existence at least from Han times, and fragments of prescriptions for the ailments of men and horses, dating from the same period, have been found at the sites of outposts on the north-west frontier. In subsequent centuries a medical profession with recognized qualifications evolved, and in 1076 a School of Medicine was founded at the Song capital, Kaifeng. These consultants, often specialists, attended to the upper class; the rest of the population consulted private practitioners of varying skills and integrity. Encyclopaedias codified medical knowledge but also helped to freeze it, so that little progress was made under the later dynasties. Nevertheless, among many dubious assertions there were remarkable discoveries such as the circulation of the blood.

The Chinese also recognized that certain diseases were caused by dietary deficiencies. Some proposed treatments were effective, although the classification of foods into 'hot' (spiced or cooked at a high temperature), 'neutral' and 'cold' (moist and green) was not much to the point. An emphasis on balance or harmony was typical of the Chinese attitude to the cosmos, and probably explains why dissection was never systematically practiced, knowledge of anatomy remained relatively limited, and surgery was hardly used except for the creation of castrati. Instead, in what would now be called a holistic approach, the body was viewed as a system of inter-relationships and a network of channels through which vital forces flowed. When not caused by spiteful demons or neglected ancestors, illness was the result of relationships which had been disrupted or channels that had become blocked. More specifically, corporeal harmony depended upon sets of correspondences which linked the five elements (water, wood, fire, earth and metal) with the five major organs of the body, and on the creative tension that existed between two fundamental life principles, yin and yang (among other things, female and male, passive and active, dark and light).

These concepts underlay the prescription of many drugs and the practice of Chinese therapies that have recently become well-known in the West. Acupuncture is at least 2,000 years old and perhaps much older. Its practitioners treat illness by inserting needles just below the surface of the skin at various precisely designated points on the body; since the body is said to be a network of twelve main and numerous subsidiary meridians (lines along which the vital forces flow), the needles may be inserted at points far from the apparently afflicted area. Although it is difficult to measure the effectiveness of treatment by acupuncture, there is no disputing the extreme sensations often experienced by those who undergo it, or the continued use of the technique in Chinese hospitals as an anaesthetic which enables the patient to remain conscious and undrugged throughout a serious operation. Another form of treatment based on the same principles, moxibustion, involves burnt sticks of mugwort (moxa), which are applied while still hot to the designated points.

Above: a talisman intended to afford protection and bring good luck to its possessor. It shows an Immortal, Liu Hai, and, above, an Eight Trigram emblem with the yin-yang, symbol of the dualities of the universe, at its centre.

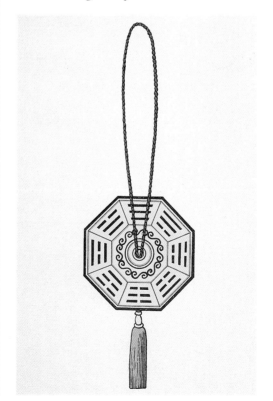

Left: amulet of Eight Trigrams, worn for good luck by Chinese children. Each of the eight panels contains a different pattern of broken and unbroken lines. The Eight Trigrams are attributed to a mythical ancestor-figure, Fuxi.

THE MIGHTY DEAD

A Chinese family greeted the death of one of its members with an outpouring of grief. This was one occasion on which the Confucian reverence for the family overrode the Confucian obligation to behave with stoicism and restraint in all circumstances; however, it is true that the most extravagant displays of emotion were assigned to the womenfolk. The death of a parent was a particularly harrowing event, and officials were expected to observe a mourning period of three years during which their salaries continued to be paid. For most literati this proved an opportunity to pursue cultivated leisure activities or extend the family's local influence, but for the ambitious man, close to the centre of power, it constituted an unforeseen sentence of exile.

For most of human history, death has been much more than an occasion for personal grief or fellow-feeling. Cultures at every stage of development have believed that the dead live on or, possessing the power to help or harm those who remain behind, have to be propitiated. In China, reverence towards ancestors was a pious duty but also a matter of prudence. The correct positioning of the grave was a vital matter, since the ancestral bones carried a powerful yin (negative) charge which had to be counteracted by the yang (positive) qualities of the burial site; those who could afford it made such decisions after taking the advice of an expert in feng-shui, the study of auspicious locations and alignments. If graves were not kept tidy and regular offerings made, the ancestors were apt to become resentful and visit ill-fortune on the offenders.

From very early times the wealthy and powerful, determined not to be forgotten, erected huge, highly visible mounds over their tombs. They also made sure that they would lack for no comfort or pleasure in the afterlife that they had known in the world above. The tombs of the Shang kings, like those of the pharaohs, were pillaged by robbers, and only traces have been found of the sculptures, vessels, weapons and chariots they once contained; but the presence of human and animal bones makes it clear that they intended to be served and guarded throughout eternity.

Under the Zhou, human sacrifices were replaced by wooden or terracotta figures, and even the cruel First Emperor was content to be protected by life-size terracotta soldiers. However, tens of thousands died in building his tomb, reputedly a microcosm of the known world; it met the fate of most such megalomaniac displays in being plundered as soon as there was a breakdown in law and order. Excavation of the area around the tomb built for the Han emperor Jangdi (156–140 BC) has uncovered the bones of thousands of labourers, proving that work on these monuments was as bad for the health as legends claimed. By Jangdi's time the movement away from literalism had gone a stage further, and the soldiers of the emperor's pottery army were only some 60 cm tall; despite differences in facial expression, they are now reminiscent of old dolls or ninepins, having lost both their silk clothes and their wooden arms. The pits associated with this imperial army also contained many animal figures and a substantial granary.

The imperial tombs proper have not been excavated, but some idea of their grandeur can be gained from the princely tomb of Liu Sheng and his wife, consisting of deep, rock-cut chambers with furnished side-galleries. The couple had evidently hoped to survive in the flesh, encasing their bodies from head to foot in fantastic suits made from thin plates of jade; in the end, it was the suits that survived. Another princely burial, though looted, was even grander in conception, with a full suite of rooms including a kitchen, a well, an ice cellar and a lavatory. The decoration and contents of Han tombs constitute most of the surviving evidence about Chinese art of the period, and their bronze and ceramic figures offer a lively account of everyday life. This is also true of the Tang period, but by the end of the dynasty tomb furnishing had diminished greatly in importance. Outward impressiveness remained the rule, especially for imperial interments, reaching something of a climax in the great processional way and surface building complexes of the Ming.

3 CONDUCT AND BELIEF

THE CHINESE WAY OF LIFE WAS BASED ON A FUSION OF TRADITION AND ETHICS THAT BOUND TOGETHER INDIVIDUALS, FAMILIES AND COMMUNITIES. ENDORSED AND DEVELOPED BY THE PHILOSOPHER CONFUCIUS AND HIS SCHOOL, THIS SOCIAL AND ETHICAL OUTLOOK PERMEATED CHINESE INSTITUTIONS. IT ALSO INFLUENCED ATTITUDES TOWARDS RELIGION AND SPIRITUAL CONCERNS, WHICH WESTERNERS GENERALLY PLACE IN A SEPARATE CATEGORY. TO THE CHINESE THE DISTINCTION WAS LESS CLEAR-CUT. THEIR WORLD WAS POPULATED BY A MULTITUDE OF DEITIES, SPIRITS, GHOSTS AND DEMONS, BUT THESE WERE APPROACHED, AS WERE A FAMILY'S OWN ANCESTORS, IN A RATHER MATTER-OF-FACT FASHION, AS ENTITIES THAT HAD TO BE PLACATED BECAUSE THEY WERE DANGEROUS, OR WERE WORTH MAKING OFFERINGS TO BECAUSE THEY COULD GRANT WISHES AND BRING GOOD FORTUNE. THE CHINESE TOOK A PRACTICAL, ECLECTIC, NON-EXCLUSIVE ATTITUDE TOWARDS SUCH OTHERWORLDLY POWERS, AND THIS WAS GENERALLY TRUE EVEN FOR THE ADHERENTS OF MORE EMOTIONAL, INWARD FAITHS SUCH AS DAOISM AND BUDDHISM.

CONFUCIUS

The western name for China's greatest sage is Confucius, a Latinized form of Kong Fuzi, 'Master Kong'. He lived (551–479 BC) during the Spring and Autumn period, when the Zhou dynasty exercised only a nominal authority and the Yellow River heartland of Chinese civilization was divided into a number of small states, almost continuously at war with one another. Confucius felt strongly that the times were out of joint, and his teachings were designed to lead the Chinese back to the superior practices of the earlier Zhou period, which Confucius believed (rightly or wrongly) to have been a golden age of order and righteous rule.

Little is known of Confucius' life. He was born in the small state of Lu, and probably belonged to the class of minor nobility or gentry that was becoming impoverished during the Spring and Autumn period, and was consequently seeking paid official posts. Confucius himself seems not to have risen very high in the service of Lu; and when, in old age, he visited other courts in order to give rulers the benefit of his mature thought, he found none willing to employ him. Like many other prophets and reformers, he was a failure in his own time. But his teachings were transmitted orally through his disciples (some of whom became distinguished statesmen), and the sage's own words were recorded in the volume known as the *Analects*. The sayings in the *Analects* are the pithily expressed judgements of an accepted master, not a reasoned exposition of his ideas; however, what is missing in terms of argument is made up for in the expression of a personality, still quite distinctive after two and a half millennia.

Seeing himself as one who wished to restore the past rather than innovate, Confucius advo-

cated the performance of all the traditional rituals. But he had no interest in discussing gods, spirits or the afterlife, insisting that it was quite difficult enough to solve problems on the human level without venturing into metaphysics. Many later Confucian literati followed the sage's example, openly expressing their scepticism about the efficacy of the rites and sacrifices which they continued to perform with punctilio.

Confucius approved of such practices because they were socially useful, and none more so than ancestor-worship, which extended into the afterlife the hierarchical principle on which the family was organized. Such hierarchies, with their fixed roles and relationships, were what held society together. Each person must perform his (and her) part: pithily expressed by eight monosyllables in the original Chinese, one of Confucius' famous sayings was 'Let the ruler rule, the minister administer, the father be a father, the son a son.' This would have been a banal endorsement of existing authority if Confucius had not also insisted that in each role – ruler, minister, father, son – a person must behave dutifully and

Above: portrait of Confucius, carved during the Tang period on a stone slab. The sage lives on as a personality, his actual words recorded in a classic volume known as the Analects.

Opposite: Confucius and his disciples, in an 18th-century painting much less severe in mood than the portrait above. The sage's disciples played a decisive role in spreading his teachings.

Confucius consults the *I Ching*. The picture is a charming Western fantasy in which the sage consults China's famous prophetic text, throwing yarrow stalks to locate a relevant passage.

benevolently: only then would harmony prevail. Advocating universal benevolence, Confucius enunciated the principle: 'Do not impose on others that which you yourself do not desire.'

The political implication was that the ruler had a right to respect and obedience, but also a duty to act justly, in the best interests of his subjects. In fact Confucian doctrine emphasized the obligations of those in authority. 'The people are like grass, the ruler is like the wind': if the ruler

set a good example, the people would follow it. A similar principle operated at other levels, including that of the literati who eventually became such a force in the Chinese state. The 'superior man' evoked by Confucius was obliged to practise self-cultivation, to preserve a calm, benevolent demeanour and to behave righteously; whereas only a more restricted range of virtues was incumbent on his inferiors. In this way Confucianism emphasized the moral responsibility that accompanied authority, while remaining a fundamentally conservative doctrine designed to shore up the existing order. At his best, the Confucian official strove to live up to the ideal of the superior man, and its very existence profoundly influenced the character of China's distinctive ruling class.

Many schools of philosophy are said to have flourished in the late Zhou period, but thanks to the Qin emperor's 'Burning of the Books' only a limited number of works have survived. Around 450 BC, Mo Zi developed a quasi-religious doctrine of universal love (shorn of its Confucian-traditionalist features such as family piety) and heavenly reward and retribution. A radically different, epicurean philosophy is associated with the shadowy figure of Yang Zhu, who seems to have advocated a quiet life of personal fulfilment, lived away from the dangerous centres of political power; in such circumstances prudence and moderation would ensure longevity.

All of these doctrines can be interpreted as responses to the insecurity of the late Zhou period: according to their temperaments, the sages recommended renovation of the state or withdrawal into private life. A sense of crisis, and belief in a political restoration, appear explicitly in the writings of Confucius' followers. The best-known of them, Mencius (Latinization of Meng Ke, c. 370–c. 290 BC), declared that the ruler who adopted Confucius' ideas would be certain to unite the Warring States. The philosopher travelled from court to court in search of such a man, but never found him.

China was not united by Confucius or in anything like the Confucian spirit. The ministers who guided Qin to victory in the 3rd century BC belonged to the Legalist school and put its tenets into practice with ruthless efficiency. Legalism was in fact more notable for its practitioners than for any philosophical formulation of its outlook; and this was appropriate, since it was above all a doctrine of action, using success as its sole criterion. Legalists put the interests of the state above everything else. Consequently they advocated a central authority with absolute power and laws that recognized no privileged persons or groups; ferocious penalties for the slightest infringement would ensure submission and obedience.

As in European states based on similar doctrines of force and expediency, Legalist ministers were usually among the victims of the system they served, and in theory should have applauded their own destruction at an expedient moment. The Legalist Qin state also resembled certain 20th-century regimes in scoring impressive military and political successes and carrying out titanic public projects before being undermined by megalomania and finally destroyed.

A state based on terror was bound to fail in the long run, as the Qin's successors recognized. The Han embraced a revived Confucianism, with its emphasis on mutual responsibilities, right conduct and traditional loyalties. Legalism was utterly discredited by the memory of Qin oppression, but of course it lived on informally, in the sense that expediency, force and fear are rarely absent from politics for long. Confucianism subsequently experienced changing fortunes, being abandoned even by many of the official class during the period when Buddhist fervour was at its height (4th–8th centuries AD). But under the Song, the triumph of the scholar-gentry ensured the supremacy of Confucian values; from this time, although different schools and interpretations arose within the Confucian tradition, its essential values were to remain unchallenged in the social sphere, right down to the end of imperial China.

Legalist philosophy in action: the bastinado (beating the soles of the feet), a painful and disabling punishment. Legalists believed that force and fear alone maintained political authority.

The Seven Sages of the Bamboo Grove. In this 20th-century ink painting on silk, the artist creates a suitably dreamlike atmosphere to evoke these literary figures of popular myth, who were believed to have conferred regularly in a bamboo grove.

POPULAR RELIGION

Unlike their master, many Confucians were inclined to scoff at the vagaries of popular cults, though publicly they upheld any that did not threaten the stability of the social order. The cults were not only bewildering in their variety but seem not to have been inspired by any organizing principle, however remote. China did have a mythical cosmology in which the principal creator, Pangu, was born from the egg of Chaos; on his death, Pangu's body became the earth and his fleas its human inhabitants. A series of sovereigns were credited with devising all the important elements of human society from agriculture to writing, and the foundation of imperial China was backdated and attributed to a pre-Xia 'Yellow Emperor'. Belief in some sort of afterlife was universal, but popular images of heaven and the underworld varied except in one point: their workings resembled those of the imperial court, and arbitrary decisions, bureaucratic blunders and red tape abounded. Evidently based on common experience, this view from below casts

China's often-admired system of government in a rather less flattering light.

If there was anything that could be described as a state religion, it was the imperial cult. This involved a series of grand ceremonies that were performed in order to inaugurate the seasons, ensure a good harvest, honour Heaven and Earth, and, in times of drought, flood or famine, placate the appropriate deities. These were lavish public spectacles, designed to entertain the people and impress them with the emperor's godlike being, but they were also remote from the people and their concerns.

Everyday worship was determined by a variety of factors including place, time and status. Many gods and spirits were regional or commercial, representing anything from a river or spring to some worthy or hero whose local fame had led to his supernatural promotion. Generally speaking, 'worship' meant making offerings to avoid natural or personal disasters or to secure the help of a god or spirit: applying in the right quarter would secure a good harvest, avert floods, recover lost property or ensure an examination pass.

The most immediate objects of worship were the supernatural powers connected with the home and family. Almost every part of the house and every activity within it was associated with a god or tutelary spirit. And in the most honoured place, on the altar of the living room, stood a tablet that held the names of several generations of the paternal ancestors; if they were not given the appropriate ritual attentions they might become spiteful, and if offerings were not made at their graves their ghosts would wander abroad in search of nourishment. Yet in their practical way the Chinese habitually revised the list of ancestors on the altar when a new death occurred in the family, adding the name of the deceased and removing that of the most distant ancestor; evidently time diminished the powers – and the hunger – of the dead, or they were expected to understand that an ordinary family's resources were limited, so that only so much attention and so many offerings could be forthcoming. For the families of the rich it was different: entire halls or sanctuaries were dedicated to ancestors, and leaving an estate large enough to fund their mainte-

nance was a certain way for an individual to perpetuate his name. The most solemn and lavish rituals of ancestor-worship were of course those performed in the imperial temples, usually by the emperor in person; they were an essential feature of the imperial cult, establishing a direct link between Earth and Heaven.

One of the Daoist Immortals sitting on his three-legged toad; early 16th century, ink and colour on paper. Living in harmony with the Dao, or Way, individuals could achieve immortality and acquire strange powers.

A universal symbol: in this 17th-century painting, people of widely different ages study the yin-yang symbol, which represents eternally interacting elements in the universe such as light and dark and male and female.

WAYS AND MEANS

Although the Chinese were eclectic in their approach to religious systems, they did have a strong sense that powerful impersonal forces were at work in the world. The rise and fall of communities and individuals were interpreted as part of a cycle dominated by one of five elements (earth, wood, fire, metal, water) and a corresponding five colours (yellow, green, white, red, black). More profoundly, the entire universe moved according to the rhythm of yin and yang, whose interlocked and complementary relationship is conveyed by a well-known disc symbol in which the s-shaped line between light and dark suggests a perpetual wheel-motion in which first one and then the other half becomes uppermost. Yang and yin represent, among other things, heaven and earth, light and dark, high and low, good and evil, male and female, and hot and cold. They are engaged in an eternal struggle or, more accurately, in an eternal interaction that can never be resolved.

Like other human beings, the Chinese tried to understand the unseen powers in order to benefit from their operation. The future was being foretold by means of oracle bones in pre-Shang times, and this form of divination became a regular feature of Shang royal ritual before becoming common at village level. The cracks that appeared on heated bones or turtle shells were interpreted as the answers to questions about future events. More sophisticated information, related to an individual's character and destiny, could be obtained from the *I Ching* or *Book of Changes*. Having gathered and discarded the stalks of yarrow plants according to a preordained procedure, the diviner interpreted the result as either a complete or broken line. The procedure was repeated until he had arrived at an arrangement of six lines (a hexagram) whose pattern of unbroken and broken lines corresponded to one of the sixty-four hexagrams in the *I Ching*; the oracular commentary accompanying the hexagram supplied the analysis or prediction required.

A more sophisticated recipe for well-being involved putting oneself in harmony with the cosmic forces rather than attempting to manipulate them. Like acupuncture and related medical treatments, feng-shui, 'wind and water' lore, was based on identifying natural lines of energy, in this case the lines running through the earth. The correct orientation of a house, determined by an expert, could bring prosperity to a family, and the siting of a grave might make the difference between benevolent influences brought to bear on the deceased's descendants and hauntings by a restless, malevolently influenced ghost.

Living in harmony with cosmic forces was also the central concept in Daoism. This was the most important native-grown Chinese religion, although even here the term has to be used without many of its western implications such as a fixed body of doctrine, an ecclesiastic hierarchy with authority over its flock, and an exclusive attitude towards other creeds. In their earliest, classic form Daoist doctrines are to be found in the *Dao De Jing* (c. 300 BC), the 'Book of the Way' said to have been written by Laozi, a founder-sage, ultimately deified, who may have been an entirely mythical figure. The Dao, or Way, was an unseen, all-pervasive reality or principle. The wise man sought to live in accordance with the Dao, avoiding futile struggle; this often entailed masterly inactivity and 'following the grain of the Universe'. Where Confucians lived according to the precepts of their master and attempted to regulate life in the world, Daoists took their cue from nature and emphasized intuition and spontaneity. The two philosophies or religions appeared to be in direct opposition, but many Chinese found it possible to reconcile and combine them in yin-yang fashion, following the doctrine that seemed appropriate to a given time or place. Thus it was said that the ideal scholar-gentleman was a Confucian in town, functioning in an official capacity, and a Daoist when living in retirement in the country.

Later on Daoism absorbed many folk-belief and magical elements, developing into a religion with priests, monasteries and liturgical texts in competition with its foreign rival, Buddhism. These two were certainly not complementary – which did not prevent ordinary Chinese from utilizing elements of both with their habitual unconcern for doctrinal rigour. Daoism was always the more strongly magic-oriented, with a particular leaning towards alchemy and recipes for immortality; these brought Daoists high imperial favour and deep disgrace, depending on whether the emperor in question was sampling the elixirs or suffering their often fatal effect.

A bronze statuette of the Daoist sage Laozi, mounted on a buffalo. This was said to have been how he left China and vanished into the west, so he is often shown in this way. In time Laozi was worshipped as a god.

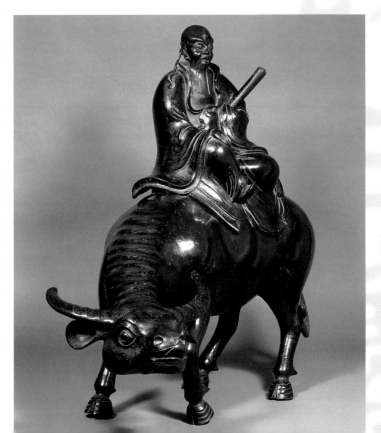

Right: Buddhist temple at
Kunming in the south-west of
China. Buddhism was the only
foreign religion that deeply
influenced the Chinese way of life.
Many Chinese took over elements
from Confucianism, Daoism and
Buddhism.

Opposite: the Buddha preaching
on Vulture Mountain; 12th-century
painting. Compassion was a
central value of Buddhism, linking
the many sects and diverse
religious practices which evolved
as it spread.

BUDDHISM

The greatest foreign influence on life in imperial China was the Buddhist religion which originated in northern India. Its founder, Siddharta Gautama, was a prince in the 6th century BC who renounced power and pleasure in order to seek the truth about life, death and suffering. When it was finally revealed to him, he became the Buddha, or Enlightened One. His basic doctrine was that suffering was unavoidable in a life dominated by desire, and that only by cultivating non-attachment could the individual hope to escape the cycle of birth and rebirth (reincarnation) and achieve the blissful state known as nirvana. Compassion was a central Buddhist value, and the performance of good works also helped the believer on the way to enlightenment. However, in time rival Buddhist schools developed, differing in the emphasis they placed on the duties of self-redemption and saving others, and proclaiming the importance of certain rituals and the existence of various deities and spiritual beings. Consequently Buddhism was already a complex creed when it began to reach China via the oases of Central Asia, probably in the 1st century AD. At first it was confined to foreign residents in China, but after the collapse of the Han it made rapid progress, the doctrine of world-rejection holding a strong appeal in an age of turmoil. As wealthy and powerful Buddhist communities developed under the Northern Wei and the Tang, lavish imperial patronage was occasionally interrupted by ferocious persecutions. Some of these were prompted by Daoist jealousy, but there were also more material reasons, including suspicion of Buddhism as a potential focus of political dissent and resentment of the way in which the exemption of monks and nuns from taxation was abused by thousands of people who had themselves ordained and then went on with ordinary family (but tax-free) lives.

Having reached China piecemeal and over vast distances, Buddhist concepts often seemed obscure and were not made any more coherent by being translated into Daoist or similarly familiar

Buddhist literature, the Chinese had already begun to adapt the faith to their own needs. The main form of Buddhism that reached China was the Mahayana ('Greater Vehicle'), which held that a series of enlightened souls, or Bodhisattvas, had put off their own entry into nirvana in order to save others; these soon became, in effect, deities for whose intercession the believer hoped and prayed. Mahayana Buddhism offered a more popular and personalized doctrine than the earlier, more austere Hinayana ('Lesser Vehicle'), and this aspect was further developed in China. Perhaps the most striking example was the transformation of an Indian male Bodhisattva, Avalokitesvara, into Guanyin, a goddess of mercy who was often represented as holding a baby in her arms; the similarity between Guanyin and Christian images of the Virgin and Child has frequently been commented on. The goddess was one of the most revered deities in Pure Land Buddhism, a Chinese sect, founded in the 5th century AD, that outstripped all other Chinese versions of Buddhism in popularity. It centred on Amitabha, the Buddha of Endless Light, who ruled over a western paradise known as The Pure Land. Dispensing with austerities and elaborate rituals, Pure Land Buddhism promised entry into the western paradise to any true believer; although the performance of simple devotions was normally expected, in extremis merely to call upon the name of Amitabha was enough to ensure salvation. In this way, Chinese Buddhism completed the evolution of the creed, which had already begun in India, from one of individual self-perfection to a universal salvationist religion.

However, other schools of Buddhism also flourished. Most Chinese monks belonged to the Chan sect, better known in the West under its Japanese name, Zen. Believing that the world was an illusion from which the individual could only be liberated by an unexpected thunderclap of revelation, the Chan master resorted to verbal paradoxes and even physical assaults to awaken his disciples to the truth.

Between the 5th and 9th centuries Buddhist fervour was at its height in China, introducing new forms and concepts into Chinese life and creating splendid, often colossal works of religious

The head of a Bodhisattva, an enlightened being who chose to remain on earth in order to help others to attain salvation. In this piece, working on soft sandstone, the sculptor was able to carve many fine details.

terms. During the cosmopolitan Tang era the long journey to India, though arduous, was not impossible for the resolute pilgrim. The most celebrated of these was the 7th-century monk Xuanzang (also known by the Indian name Tripitaka), whose adventures supply the pretext for the famous novel *Journey to the West* (Monkey); Xuanzang was able to bring back a large portfolio of Buddhist texts, and subsequently translated most of them accurately into Chinese. Although this supplied a large and reliable corpus of

art. For a time, Buddhism seemed to have eclipsed Confucianism and to be becoming the predominant Chinese religion. The turning-point was reached in 844–5 when the Tang Emperor Wu introduced progressively more stringent legislation, drastically reducing the permissible number of temples and shrines and defrocking all but the most elderly monks and nuns. Wu died in 846, possibly as a result of over-dosing on Daoist elixirs, and his successor reversed many of his decrees; yet from about this time Buddhist belief lost something of its fervour. While remaining popular, it ceased to have such an exclusive appeal and tended to be absorbed into the polytheistic patchwork of Chinese religious life. But if, for many Chinese, the Buddha became only one deity among many, the iconography, the ceremonies and above all the inwardness and compassionate attitudes of Buddhism had a permanent influence on many aspects of imperial China.

One other feature of Chinese Buddhism, not easy to understand, is the way in which it became associated with secret societies, and in particular with cults committed to revolution and the inauguration of an egalitarian golden age. Part of the explanation lies in the appeal of Maitreya, the Buddha of the Future, when viewed not as a Bodhisattva destined to be the next in the line of Buddhas, but as a world-saving figure; this was his role in the eschatology of, among others, the White Lotus sect which posed a severe challenge to the Manchus at the end of the 18th century. Buddhism may well have had a special appeal to the outsider elements in Chinese society because it gave little weight to the social advantages they lacked: a defined role and a place in the family and clan structures upheld by Confucians. Buddhist elevation of celibacy and preoccupation with the individual soul were certainly characteristics that many Confucian literati found objectionable; to them celibacy was doubly anti-social because it rejected the family and denied ancestors the future generations of worshippers that were essential to their well-being. Significantly, in the faction-fights that took place at the imperial court, the eunuchs were often associated with Buddhism in opposition to the Confucian official class.

Guanyin, Buddhist goddess of mercy; Yuan dynasty porcelain. Originally a male Bodhisattva, in China Guanyin became a potent female divinity and a distinctive Chinese contribution to Buddhism.

4 THE MANDATE OF HEAVEN

WHEN EUROPEANS BEGAN TO FIND OUT ABOUT THE CHINESE EMPIRE, THEY WERE DEEPLY IMPRESSED BY ITS SIZE AND LONGEVITY. BUT THEY WERE MOST STRUCK BY WHAT THEY TOOK TO BE ITS SUPREMELY RATIONAL FORM OF GOVERNMENT. THE AUTOCRATIC, DIVINELY ORDAINED POWER OF THE EMPEROR AND THE SPLENDOUR OF HIS COURT WERE EXOTIC VARIATIONS ON DESPOTISMS THAT HAD EXISTED IN MANY PLACES SINCE ANTIQUITY. BUT THERE WAS NO PRECEDENT FOR A STATE RUN BY CIVIL SERVANTS WHO HAD QUALIFIED FOR OFFICE BY TAKING EXAMINATIONS. NOTIONS ABOUT RATIONAL POLITICAL ARRANGEMENTS, PARTLY INSPIRED BY THE CHINESE EXAMPLE, HAD A PROFOUND INFLUENCE ON EUROPEAN MOVEMENTS IN FAVOUR OF REFORM. LATER AND MORE SOUNDLY BASED INVESTIGATIONS HAVE MODIFIED SUCH VIEWS OF IMPERIAL GOVERNMENT, YET THE DURABILITY OF THE EMPIRE AND ITS INSTITUTIONS REMAINS A FACT OF HISTORY. A DYNASTY MIGHT FALL, BUT THANKS TO THE CONCEPT OF THE MANDATE OF HEAVEN, ITS REPLACEMENT COULD BE ACCEPTED AS LEGITIMATE AS SOON AS ITS HOLD ON POWER WAS UNMISTAKABLE. CHINESE HISTORY APPEARED TO FOLLOW CYCLICAL LAWS, AND THE CELESTIAL EMPIRE WOULD, IT SEEMED, LAST FOR EVER.

The Sui emperor Yangdi strolls in his gardens with his harem; 17th-century painting on silk. While he enjoyed the 'Mandate of Heaven' the emperor was regarded as a semi-divine being.

THE DRAGON THRONE

The Imperial seal; this 18th-century example is made of jade. An order sent in the name of the emperor – even an order to commit suicide – had to be instantly obeyed, on pain of unimaginably severe torments.

In China, the emperor was the supreme authority. Sovereigns were usually surrounded by ministers and officials whose advice and criticism was conventionally regarded as carrying great weight; but ultimately imperial rule was completely autocratic and unlimited. A good many sovereigns flaunted the fact by purges and massacres of which the privileged – close blood relations, nobles and mandarins – were often the prime targets. Few of the victims put up any resistance or attempted to flee, and for many of them a message from the emperor was sufficient to elicit an obedient suicide. Moreover conspiracies aimed at removing an unstable or arbitrary emperor were remarkably rare, despite the intrigues that multiplied in the closed world of the palace. Though legal codes governed ordinary judicial proceedings in the Celestial Empire, the Son of Heaven had an overriding power of life and death over his subjects that seems to have been accepted without question, even by officials whose functions included criticizing the propriety or political wisdom of that same emperor's policies.

All this suggests that the divine attributes of the emperor were taken very seriously and that to submit to his will was much the same as submitting to the will of Heaven. (The link seems even stronger when it is recalled that most Chinese visualized Heaven as a kind of imperial court, not infrequently characterized by arbitrary acts and bureaucratic errors.) The term 'Son of Heaven' was used, long before the foundation of the empire, to describe the Shang rulers, who were present at regular divination ceremonies and often seem to have presided over them, playing, at the very least, a quasi-priestly role in the proceedings. A concept of sacred kingship also seems to underlie the position of the Zhou kings during the Warring States period, politically impotent yet revered and even subsidized by more powerful rulers, whose own eminence was justified by their real or affected blood-relationship with the king. Finally, the first Qin emperor acquired, and made full use of, a terrifying power over all his subjects, bringing back together the secular and semi-divine functions of sovereignty.

The sacredness of the imperial person was emphasized by the seclusion in which he dwelt and the ceremonial that surrounded his actions, even in private. Those admitted to his presence

Kangxi, the first great Qing emperor, on tour in 1699. This outward-going sovereign's activities contrasted with those of so many of his predecessors, sequestered behind palace walls.

carried out the obligatory 'kowtow' (pinyin *koutou*), consisting of 'three kneelings and nine prostrations'. Like such western equivalents as the curtsey, the kowtow could be performed by practiced officials and courtiers with a certain dignified economy that somewhat reduced its humiliating aspect; whereas when, in 1793, Dutch envoys attempted it at the court of Qianlong, their efforts gave rise to general hilarity. However, ideas of dignity are relative, and outsiders experienced not dissimilar feelings of amusement on viewing the way Chinese courtiers scampered about, since it was not permitted to walk in the presence of the Son of Heaven.

Most of the emperor's public appearances had a religious, or at least ritualistic, dimension. He took the central role in a series of performances that were designed to impress the populace as spectacles and pictured the sovereign as responsible for maintaining the order of the universe; hence he inaugurated the calendar and the seasons and sacrificed to Heaven, Earth and the imperial ancestors. When droughts and other calamities

threatened, he led prayers for Heaven to show mercy, and during really serious crises he might issue an edict taking the blame for the injustices on earth that had raised the wrath of the powers above; whether sincere or otherwise, such self-condemnation served to make clear the uniqueness of imperial responsibility.

The autocratic power and sacred functions of the emperor should in theory have made him secure and untouchable, but of course they did no such thing. The divine right of kings was a doctrine well known in the West, where its credibility was all too often undermined by the impunity with which sovereigns and dynasties were removed and replaced. The Chinese resolved the intellectual difficulty by the way in which they interpreted the Mandate of Heaven, or divine authority to rule. The Mandate conferred an absolute authority, but it could be withdrawn from a sovereign whose conduct was unworthy and angered Heaven; and, in keeping with Chinese ideas of collective responsibility, the emperor's downfall involved that of his entire line. The passing of the Mandate manifested itself in clusters of misfortunes: ineffective and corrupt government, barbarian invasions, revolts by powerful provincial governors or military men, peasant uprisings and droughts, floods and famines.

To the sceptical outsider, the Mandate doctrine looks like pure pragmatism, equating legitimacy with success and moral turpitude with defeat: the strong emperor is legitimate and mandated; the emperor whose power is slipping away has – must have – forfeited the Mandate and any claim to legitimacy and obedience. Similarly, the rebel either deserves a humiliating death or has recognized the will of Heaven, depending on the outcome of his rebellion. This was not, however, as the Chinese saw things, and in one respect at least, Heaven was believed to speak: a future emperor was said to be surrounded by a coloured mist which made it possible to identify him; presumably this increased the culpability of those who could not see an unmistakable sign from heaven or wilfully chose to ignore it. One of the limitations of traditional Chinese historical writing stemmed from acceptance of the Mandate principle: the foundation and collapse of dynasties could only be discussed in terms of stereotypical imperial personalities, since it was axiomatic that the final sovereign of a failing dynasty was unworthy and his destined successor strong and virtuous. Nevertheless, the Mandate theory represented a far from despicable effort by the Chinese to understand the past and make sense of the ups and downs of history; if the facts sometimes had to be interpreted a little implausibly in order to fit into its framework, the same can be said of a good many historical theories.

A phoenix robe that belonged to the late-19th-century Empress Dowager Cixi. The phoenix was one of the four guardians of the Celestial Empire.

Imperial chariot; part of the Terracotta Army buried close to the tomb of the First Emperor, who died in 210 BC. Unlike most of the chariots in the burial pits, this one is closed in, perhaps to afford greater protection to the eminent person inside.

THE STATE

Good government has rarely been achieved anywhere for very long, and any history of China will include a fairly lengthy list of weak or foolhardy emperors, corrupt institutions and misjudged political and economic crises. But when this fact has been admitted, the political and social achievements of the Chinese remain impressive. For most of the 2,000-year imperial period their land, more like a continent than a nation-state, was a single political unit, run by a qualified class of officials under the direction of an all-powerful emperor or his surrogate. Although dynastic ups and downs in an encapsulated account of Chinese history, the long periods of good order and stability, and the durability of political and social arrangements over the millennia, are actually more striking phenomena. The details of central government arrangements changed from dynasty to dynasty, but a basic hierarchical structure was maintained from first to last. One or two outstanding advisers were in charge of the bodies appointed to formulate policy, while half-a-dozen ministers or boards controlled major areas of concern such as finance; lesser issues were dealt with by ad hoc agencies.

One remarkable institution, the Censorate, was specifically charged with investigating the way in which the government functioned and submitting critical reports on it. The effects of such investigations in checking abuses and keeping alive debates on policy are hard to assess, but they must have counteracted some of the dangers of a system in which the sovereign was remote from everyday realities and bureaucratic procedures tended to become increasingly convoluted and inefficient. For very long periods the

Censorate and similar auxiliary bodies carried out their functions without provoking imperial resentment; but when things went awry at the heart of the system, it became dangerous to reveal (for example) the peculations of a corrupt favourite or to denounce the oppressive policies of a powerful eunuch who controlled access to the emperor. However, the tradition of scholarly forthrightness was very strong, and state records show that there were courageous officials at most times who were prepared to risk the terrible consequences rather than remain silent. The existence of such records, self-derogatory as well as self-glorifying, illustrates the passion for paperwork that became such a feature of the Confucian official mentality, with mixed consequences so far as good government was concerned.

Provincial governors, prefects in charge of smaller areas and a host of other officials represented the central authorities at local level. Their activities were controlled by a mass of regulations, and their relations with the populace at times suggested that the authorities hoped to control every aspect of life in totalitarian fashion. But it would be more accurate to say that they did everything they could to maintain the status quo. Imperial China's order and stability was not an accident but the highest priority of policy. Change was threatening to authority in a society with (by modern standards) limited resources and poor communications; the Confucian tradition, with its reverence for ancestors and cult of the classics, was inherently conservative. Foreign contacts were viewed with suspicion because of their disruptive potential, and one reason for Confucians' hostility towards merchants was that their activities changed tastes and attitudes and subverted the notion of a fixed social order. Had it been possible, China's rulers would have perpetuated an immobile society in which every person knew and accepted his, and her, place. This ideal is now usually dismissed as depressingly undynamic, but it has in fact been held by most preindustrial societies; and it is perhaps not axiomatic that progress (with or without inverted commas) increases the sum of human happiness.

In practice, government combined paternalistic activity with the encouragement of a moni-

tored local autonomy. The state constructed defences, canals and roads. It issued coins, conducted censuses, established monopolies, collected taxes and exacted labour services on public works. For several centuries it even tried to control the distribution of land-holding, insisting that every farmer had an area to cultivate that was

A Tang government official, portrayed in a typical pose of calm superiority; pottery tomb figure. An all-encompassing bureaucracy was the means by which the vast and varied Chinese empire was held together.

A page illustrating the costumes, accessories and modes of travel of the official class under the Qing dynasty. The chair shown here is a humbler object, affording less privacy, than the impressive sedan featured on page 97.

commensurate with the labour resources available to him. This 'equal field policy' would have helped poorer families, but seems never to have been successfully enforced outside areas of state-sponsored new settlement, doubtless because local landlords wielded too much influence to be challenged by officials. Consequently, in the course of the Tang era administrators gave up the attempt and allowed a free market in land. However, dispossessed peasants and victims of war or natural disasters received help from the state granaries, and other relief funds and charities alleviated rural and urban distress.

This is, of course, an ideal version of how government operated in imperial China. The reality could be very different when institutions such as the charitable agencies became corrupt (as they did under the Ming) and huge sums lined the pockets of administrators rather than the destitute. Moreover, even the most upright official had to make concessions when dealing with prejudiced provincial superiors or local vested interests. And the demands of the state were carefully channelled through local associations, which became responsible for, say, ensuring that taxes were paid, but were left to go about it in their own way, undisturbed by authority unless they failed to get the required results. The idea of collective rather than individual responsibility was very strong in China (as we have seen, the fall of a minister could lead to the destruction of the entire clan to which he belonged), and a typical way of securing good behaviour was to group households into units of ten, a hundred or a thousand, and rotate a variety of duties among their heads. Failure to collect taxes or report a crime incurred communal punishment, so the group had a strong motive for ensuring that all its members behaved themselves. It also possessed the means to do so, since, outside the big cities, neighbours were likely to be well-informed about one another's affairs.

Similar arrangements ensured that the administrative system was not over-burdened with litigation. From at least Tang times, China had an impressive legal code, and among the many duties performed by mandarins were those of a magistrate. But although the official was obliged to investigate when certain offences were committed, many crimes and disputes were dealt with by the community; its members had the traditional rural distrust of outside authority, and preferred to see partial justice done rather than risk the unpredictable consequences of direct involvement with the state. Those who did so became aware of the Five Punishments that might lie at the end of the legal process: execution by decapitation or strangling, exile (commonly in the form of army service on the frontier), penal servitude, and two types of beating, depending on the severity of the offense.

Whether imposing its will on the populace or permitting them a degree of self-regulation, the imperial government was motivated above all by a wish to maintain order and avoid any kind of agitation. The imperial symbol, the dragon, was in Chinese mythology an amiable beast, and the Confucian ideal of the mandarin class emphasized benevolence; but in practice the welfare of the people was secondary to the need for security and tranquillity. To be fair, many governments beside that of imperial China have put security first and have insisted that it is the most basic form of welfare provision; the ultimate in the breakdown of order – the complete absence of social controls – was described by the 17th-century British philosopher Thomas Hobbes as a 'state of nature' in which life was inescapably 'solitary, poor,

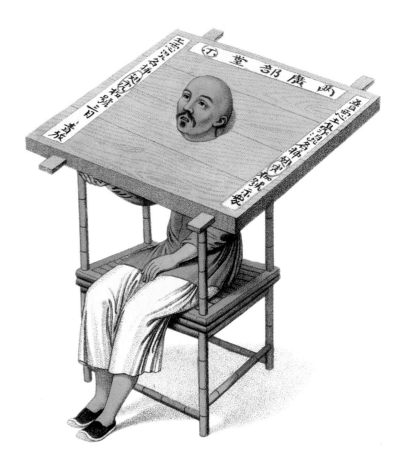

nasty, brutish and short'. But the human cost of an ordered, secure society could be very high, especially in an autocratic system where a single decree could change or sweep away thousands of lives. The Great Wall and the Grand Canal are two imperial achievements (life- rather than labour-intensive) that can only be viewed with a mixture of awe, admiration and horror. The later empire can boast an equally stringent imperial measure in the response of the newly installed Qing dynasty to the threat from pirate-rebels who constantly raided the coast from Taiwan: in 1661 they enforced the removal of the entire population from a very large coastal area, initiating a kind of 'burnt earth' policy that deprived the pirates of supplies, and perhaps of covert assistance, even though this meant making refugees of huge numbers of their subjects. Not for the last time in Chinese history, the country's rulers seem to have been guided by the harsh Daoist observation that 'Heaven and earth are ruthless, and treat all creatures like straw dogs [offerings, thrown carelessly aside after use]; the sage is ruthless, and treats the people like straw dogs.'

Condemned to wear an enormous wooden collar, this offender has been humiliated and unpleasantly constrained. However, Chinese justice dealt out many far more unpleasant punishments.

WITHIN THE COURT

The callousness often displayed by the emperors must have been encouraged by the semi-divine status of the Son of Heaven and the artificial conditions in which he was raised and lived. The sacred character of the emperor was such that he had little contact with his subjects except as a remote figure seen presiding at public ceremonies. Although the founder of a dynasty was usually a robust individual who commanded in the field and waded through blood to the throne, his descendants were brought up behind palace walls; they became enmeshed in court ritual and distracted – sometimes to the point of obsession – by the unlimited private pleasures available to the sovereign, including a harem that might have a thousand or more resident concubines. In such a situation, an emperor might still take an active role in policy-making, or might at least have the sense to rely on experienced ministers to run the empire for him; but his upbringing made it just as likely that he would put his trust in intimate but unqualified friends or servants. This kind of weakness was not of course unique to China, but

has characterized most long-established autocracies. Some Chinese emperors fell under the sway of wives or concubines; others put their confidence in favourites or palace eunuchs. Certain patterns repeated themselves over millennia, giving plausibility to the Chinese view of their history as cyclical. A woman might gain influence over an emperor, as Yang Guifei did over the aged Xuanzong; but a romantic episode of this kind (which ended by Yang Guifei being strangled at the demand of the emperor's army) was a less reliable path to power than the ability to provide the realm with an heir. The careers of the Empress Wu and the Empress Dowager Cixi were closely similar despite the fact that twelve centuries separated them: each ruled initially as the regent for her own child, using this temporary position to create an impregnable power-base.

Strangely enough, although the Chinese literati cultivated male friendship, few emperors acquired glamorous favourites of the type so often found in European history. The outstanding exception was the handsome He Shen, who

女史司箴敢告庶姬

Palace life in the 4th century AD. This is not the original of Gu Kaizhi's *Admonitions of the Instructress to the Court Ladies*; but the copy itself is the oldest Chinese painting on a handscroll to have survived.

dominated the later years of the Qing emperor Qianlong, falsifying accounts, taking bribes and behaving with imperial effrontery until Qianlong's demise brought about his own fall and self-administered death. Descriptions of He Shen, and of others, such as the eunuchs who also wielded power through imperial favour or acquiescence, suggest that these individuals lived in a feverish, unreal atmosphere, indulging in extremes of tyranny, extravagance and self-glorification, perhaps in the consciousness that their fortunes were dependent on the survival of the emperor; sooner or later his death would lead to disgrace, arrest and, at best, gracious permission to commit suicide.

In spite of this grim prospect, there was never any shortage of individuals for whom power was worth any risk. The group that most often usurped authority was the corps of palace eunuchs. They were employed to perform a range of duties in the emperor's private quarters and in any circumstances that involved contact with his empress or concubines. The mutilated condition of the eunuchs ensured that the emperor alone had access to his women, and imperial sensitivi-

ties on the point were so acute that castration was savagely thorough, involving the removal of the penis as well as the testicles; inevitably, a percentage of those subjected to the operation did not recover from it. The majority of eunuchs were the sons of poor people who had been sold as children, but some individuals actually underwent the operation in adult life in order to further their ambitions. The palace eunuchs displayed a considerable solidarity over the centuries, no doubt because of their distinctive, isolated position in a society that exalted family ties and the carrying on of a name from generation to generation. (The eunuchs themselves subscribed to the universal sentiment, taking advantage of their power during one period to acquire the right to found an artificial family through adoption.) Their solidarity strengthened the influence they wielded because of their intimacy with the imperial family, especially when the emperor had been born and had grown up within the harem.

Reliance on eunuchs was strongest among emperors with little taste for state business or the high-mindedness of the usual Confucian scholar-ministers; so eunuch power is most often associated with imperial decadence and the decline and fall of dynasties. Eunuchs appear to have played an important political role even under the Zhou, and became contenders for power under the later Han; in AD 168 they overthrew their enemies and dominated the state until 189, when it was their turn to be slaughtered. Six centuries later, under the Tang, eunuchs again emerged as trusted advisers and took on a new role as generals; one advantage of employing them was held to be that, however successfully a eunuch general performed on the battlefield, he would never be tempted to revolt and set up his own dynasty. But on occasion eunuchs did establish such a grip on the state apparatus that even the emperor feared to challenge them openly.

In the notorious Sweet Dew Incident of 835 an attempt to lure the eunuch leaders into a trap (they were induced to investigate the 'dew of immortality' said to have fallen overnight) miscarried when a breeze moved the curtain concealing the waiting assassins. Warned in time, the eunuch generals conducted a savage purge of their opponents and continued to control imperial affairs until the dynasty was overthrown and they perished at the hands of the usurper Zhu Wen.

Eunuchs were prominent at times after China was reunited by the Song, but the apogee of eunuch power was reached during the Ming period, when tens of thousands were attached to the imperial court. This was ironic, since the founder of the dynasty, Hongwu (1368–98), was aware of the danger posed by such a powerful interest group and advised that eunuchs should be prevented from becoming literate in order to make sure they were harmless. The advice was soon forgotten, and from the 15th century several individual eunuchs became effectively dictators, backed by a kind of palace secret police that was capable of terrorizing any opposition.

However, the power-mongering of the eunuchs was the result rather than the cause of late Ming decadence. The role that women could play is highlighted by intrigues at the end of Wanli's reign (1572–1620), when the old emperor's favourite, Madame Cheng, was believed to have poisoned his successor, and the mother of the new emperor, hoping to establish a regency, had to be besieged in the palace and expelled with some difficulty.

This emperor, Tianqi (1620–27), was a reputedly illiterate youth, passionate only about carpentry. His reign witnessed the ascendancy of the most hated of all the eunuch dictators, Wei Zhongxian, who established what can only be described as a personality cult during the 1620s. Those who wished to survive, let alone prosper, were obliged to flatter Wei in the grossest terms on monuments and in memorials to the throne; temples were built in his honour; and Wei's nephew even substituted for the emperor himself at a sacrifice in the imperial temple. It was rumoured that China would soon have its first eunuch sovereign, but the premature death of the emperor in 1627 led to Wei's downfall; he evaded arrest and a more painful demise by taking his own life. Significantly, the Ming dynasty came to an end less than twenty years later.

Eunuchs remained a feature of palace life under the Qing, but the new rulers were determined to learn from the mistakes of their predecessors. Though a good many follies were committed by the later Qing emperors (and by the Empress Dowager), eunuchs were never allowed the kind of political ascendancy by the Manchus that they had enjoyed under their predecessors.

Princesses of the Tang era; pottery figures from a tomb with painted and gilded details. They are fashionably turned out with elaborate hairstyles, flower-patterned gowns, huge sleeves and turned-up lotus-form shoes.

MILITARY MATTERS

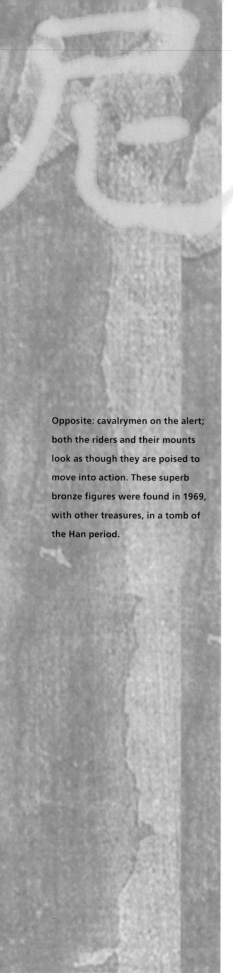

Opposite: cavalrymen on the alert; both the riders and their mounts look as though they are poised to move into action. These superb bronze figures were found in 1969, with other treasures, in a tomb of the Han period.

Over time, Chinese society was increasingly dominated by the scholar-official class, whose contempt for military men spread among other sections of the population. However, the history of imperial China is filled with bloody episodes, and it was the exploits of the imperial armies during the Qin, Han and Tang periods that transformed a group of relatively small states along the Yellow River into a mighty empire. Though important, anti-militarism was a relatively late development which did not alter the fact that relations between the state and its military servants had long been a crucial political problem.

Little is known about warfare before the Shang period, when inscriptions on oracle bones help to amplify finds from Anyang and other sites. Commanded by their semi-divine kings, Shang armies consisted of squadrons of chariots backed by foot-soldiers. The chariot was almost certainly a borrowing from the Middle East, used for rapid manoeuvering rather than crashing into the enemy in tanklike assaults (horses big and strong enough for this purpose had not yet been bred anywhere). The chariot carried a three-man team consisting of a driver, an archer and a halberdier, who cut down the opposition with scythe-like swings of his long weapon. As the elite arm, the chariots were probably manned by royal and aristocratic individuals, while the common folk, equipped with spears, knives and axes, served as arrow-fodder.

Constant wars under the Zhou provided food for thought, and about 490 BC Sun Zi wrote the first known study of *The Art of War*. By the Warring States period (464–222 BC) a series of innovations were changing the nature of conflicts. New weapons such as the sword and the crossbow were introduced, cavalry began to replace chariots, and the infantry became the core of the army. Under the Qin, the summons to fight, issued by a local lord, was replaced by systematic conscription, creating the force that would sweep away all Shi Huangdi's rivals. These men are graphically portrayed in the Terracotta Army of life-size figures, discovered after more than 2,000 years on

duty guarding the First Emperor's tomb. The bronze triggers of their (otherwise perished) crossbows and the corrosion-resistant quality of their sword-blades have provided unimpeachable evidence of the advanced state of Chinese metallurgy and military technology.

The Qin emperor built the Great Wall to defend China against the steppe nomads to the north, and the Han extended it westward to protect caravans bound for the Central Asian Silk Road. Many details of service on the Great Wall are known through the discovery of records written on wood or bamboo strips. Battlemented towers of plastered brick stood at regular intervals along the wall; useful for surveillance and defence, they also served as signal-stations from which coded messages could be sent by flags or torches. Banks of sand were laid beyond the wall so that night-marauders and spies left visible evidence of their passage. Travel across the frontier was strictly monitored, and passports had to be obtained to enter or leave China. Garrisons were highly organized, and many conscripts in practice worked as farmers and labourers to feed and house the military colony. With typical clerical thoroughness the authorities recorded the issue of equipment, the distribution of supplies and other details, although not the sense of being stranded and isolated that must have assailed conscript recruits in a northern fastness.

Under the Tang, Chinese troops were sent even further afield, deep into Central Asia. The Tang governing class was mostly drawn from the north-western warrior-aristocracy, and consequently the military values — heroism and a code of honour — were particularly cultivated. From the 1st century BC big horses had been imported from Ferghana, and cavalry had come to play a decisive role in warfare. The Tang bred horses on a large scale, and their passion for noble steeds is obvious in their painting and in the many figures of horses found in their tombs. Though conscripts took part in the great 7th-century wars of conquest, the Tang remodelled the army into a professional organization. From the 8th century until

the empire ended the population was divided into soldiers and civilians, and peasant militias were recruited only for local emergencies.

As a specialized force, the army became an alien and potentially predatory institution. This was true both for ordinary people, who were liable to be despoiled by the soldiery as soon as conditions became unstable, and for the scholar-officials whose authority was threatened whenever military men became politically powerful. Confucian values, which emphasized self-cultivation and moral rectitude, were antithetical to the active martial spirit, and by the Song period there was no doubt that the scholars' attitudes were permeating Chinese society. Yet the soldier was both necessary and dangerously difficult to control. The empire had to be defended, but a large frontier army gave an ambitious commander the means to challenge the dynasty. The problem had arisen under the Tang, when An Lushan's rebellion demonstrated that appointing a barbarian was no solution. Later dynasties would try a variety of schemes, including appointing eunuch generals, incapable of founding a dynasty, and retaining the best troops under direct imperial control close to the capital, at the risk of weakening the frontiers.

The Song solution was to keep the military under strict civilian control, subjecting them to a mass of bureaucratic regulations, forbidding even minor initiatives without authorization, and creating a network of separate commands. This worked well from a security point of view but hardly made for a flexible, high-morale force that was capable of defeating the empire's enemies. As a result, the Song never made genuinely sustained attempts to recover lost territory and, despite their defensive stance, had an unimpressive military record. Paradoxically, it was during this period that the size of the armed forces increased dramatically, becoming a serious burden on the state finances, and extraordinary innovations were introduced in military technology. A variety of catapults and other siege weapons were devised, and the first effective Chinese navy was developed. Above all, gunpowder was harnessed to make explosives, in the 11th century in the form of bombs and grenades, in the 12th as projectiles

fired from bamboo tubes. Unluckily for the Song, the Mongols quickly learned the secret of making firearms, and continued to defeat them in battle.

The Yuan were always a foreign dynasty, ruling through an army of occupation. However, the Ming emperors, who expelled and succeeded them, took over certain Mongol practices, of which the most striking was to make soldiering a hereditary occupation in certain families, who received tax and labour-service concessions in return. This was a sign of a hardening of arteries characteristic of the Ming, under whom Chinese inventiveness declined. When the Chinese were faced by superior Japanese firearms in Korea, their casting skill was not good enough for them to catch up without help from European Jesuits.

Concern for the safety of the northern frontier caused the Ming to rebuild the Great Wall, adding strategically important new stretches across the Ordos desert and the region north of the capital, Beijing. The cost of maintaining a large army was now very high, and the Ming tried to solve it by establishing self-sufficient military colonies on the frontiers. Many soldiers were effectively turned into peasants, but the colonies remained dependent on supplies from outside. These were brought in by convicts, or by merchants who accomplished the task in return for salt-manufacture concessions; they eventually realized that it was more efficient to set up their own colonies, cultivating the land and supplying the army on the spot. The system was liable to become corrupt, and the northern defences ran down in the absence of any threat. There was no equivalent recovery when the Manchus began to go from strength to strength, but it was a Chinese general who in 1644 opened the First Entrance Under Heaven and unwittingly ensured that the Ming would be China's last native dynasty.

Above: ceremonial knife with a bronze handle and jade blade. The intricate decoration includes a dragon mask, so stylized that it might be an abstract design.

Opposite: model of a well-equipped border guard of the Tang period; discovered in a shrine at a remote outpost guarding the northern Silk Road leading to Central Asia.

Below: daggers and dagger-axes from the Shang and Zhou dynasties. The oldest, turquoise-inlaid example (far left) dates from the 13th or 14th century BC.

5 THE ARTS OF CHINA

FEW CIVILIZATIONS CAN MATCH THE 4,000-YEAR RECORD OF CHINESE ARTS AND CRAFTS. TIME AND DISTANCE HAVE NOT HINDERED THE OUTSIDE WORLD FROM APPRECIATING CHINA'S VISUAL AND TACTILE ARTS – HER JADES AND SILKS, LACQUER AND PORCELAIN, PAINTED LANDSCAPES AND MYSTERIOUS BRONZES. CREATED BY A PEOPLE WHO SUFFERED MANY UPHEAVALS BUT NEVER EXPERIENCED A FUNDAMENTAL BREAK IN THEIR CULTURAL DEVELOPMENT, THESE ARTS GIVE AN IMPRESSION OF HOMOGENEITY, AS IF REFLECTING A CHINESE CHARACTER THAT WAS FORMED EARLY, PERMEATED EVERY ACTIVITY AND NEVER UNDERWENT SIGNIFICANT CHANGE. THIS IS OF COURSE A HALF-TRUTH, FOR SOME OUTSIDE INFLUENCES, NOTABLY BUDDHISM, HAD AN UNMISTAKABLE IMPACT ON THE ARTS, QUITE APART FROM THE FACT THAT CHINESE TASTES CAN BE SHOWN TO HAVE CHANGED OVER TIME. BUT THE OTHER HALF OF THE TRUTH IS THAT OUTSIDE INFLUENCES, HOWEVER STRONG, WERE ULTIMATELY ABSORBED OR TRANSFORMED, AND THAT REVERENCE FOR THE PAST DID LEAD THE CHINESE TO ADOPT A DISTINCTIVE ATTITUDE TOWARDS THE ARTS. THEY WERE ALWAYS RELUCTANT TO ABANDON ANY ESTABLISHED MOTIF, SYMBOL OR STYLE, PREFERRING TO KEEP IT IN THE REPERTOIRE AND RE-INTERPRET OR RE-WORK IT; OFTEN ENOUGH, A STRONG REVIVALIST IMPULSE WOULD LEAD TO THE CREATION OF PIOUS IMITATIONS, SO THAT FROM THE SONG PERIOD ONWARDS WEALTHY PATRONS WERE COMMISSIONING BRONZES IN THE SHANG STYLE OF 2,000 YEARS EARLIER. SUCH FACTS LEADS US TO CONCLUDE THAT THE CHINESENESS OF CHINESE ART IS, TO SAY THE LEAST, NOT ENTIRELY AN ILLUSION.

The signs of the Chinese Zodiac surrounding the yin-yang symbol; carved stone from a temple in Chengdu, Sichuan. Each creature was associated with a time of day and one year in every twelve.

ART, CRAFT AND SYMBOL

The Chinese, like the Victorians, distinguished firmly between the Fine and the Applied Arts. Painting, calligraphy and poetry were creative pursuits, practised by gentlemen of the scholar-official class. Other arts and crafts, even sculpture, were the province of manual workers; their decorative qualities were admirable, but as the product of mechanical, repetitive labour they belonged very definitely to a separate category. This view prevailed throughout the dynastic era. Needless to say, the modern tendency is to ignore such distinctions and to appreciate to the full the technical mastery, superb sense of form and delightful decorative qualities of the ceramic and other 'applied' arts.

Most Chinese art is highly accessible because it appears beautiful to the untrained eye as well as to the eye of the connoisseur. Although background information may enhance the spectator's enjoyment, it is rarely indispensable. This is true, for example, of the wealth of symbols employed, reflecting the complexity of Chinese culture and their marked taste for numbering and listing. They include the signs of the Chinese Zodiac, the Eight Precious Things, the Five Colours, and an elaborate set of correspondences between animals, season and the five elements. Daoism had its own Eight Emblems, and its obsession with longevity was reflected in the popularity of deer, stork and tortoise symbols; still higher hopes were embodied in the hare, said to live in the moon and spend its time there preparing the ingredients of the Elixir of Life. The lists and parallelisms were extended to Buddhism, which also had its Eight Emblems, including the lotus, symbol of generative power. The Chinese fondness for bouquets and blossoms is apparent in their decorative arts, and there was an entire language of flowers that eventually covered every aspect of existence, offering an alternative to animal and other symbols; to take only the most popular blooms, chrysanthemums represented happiness and a gift of narcissi or peonies was given to wish the recipient good luck.

The Chinese also excelled in the creation of

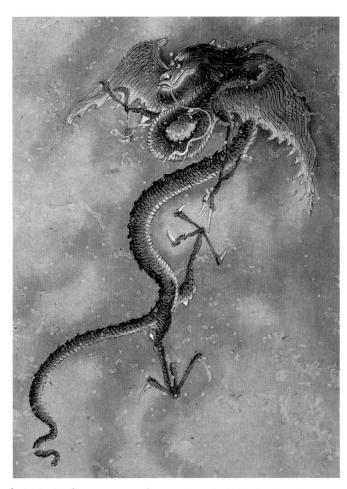

fantasy creatures, of which the dragon was easily the most potent. Unlike its western counterpart, the dragon was a benevolent beast associated with spring, life-giving rains and the harvest; more generally, it represented the life force and might be stalked by the death-figure of the tiger. These qualities make it easy to understand why the dragon became the principal imperial symbol and the current sovereign was said to occupy the Dragon Throne. Courtiers and officials were eventually permitted to imitate their master by wearing costumes decorated with dragon figures, but an element of imperial exclusiveness remained: only the imperial robes could be blazoned with dragons possessing the largest complement of claws — five — on each foot. The empress had her own symbol, often described in western literature as a phoenix, although it had no connection with the fabled Arabian bird; the Chinese 'phoenix' was a composite, combining elements of the pheasant, peacock and crane. Dragon and 'phoenix' often appear together (for example on ceramics) as joint-imperial symbols.

Fierce but friendly: this rather serpentine winged dragon comes from an album of watercolours, dated 1839; it is a fittingly vital representation of a creature seen by the Chinese as an embodiment of the life force.

The 'flying' horse. This famous figure is made of cast bronze and shows the horse borne up by a flying swallow beneath its hoof. It comes from a tomb in Gansu; later Han, 2nd century AD.

BRONZES

The Bronze Age in China began in the late 18th century BC, or perhaps a century or two before. The earliest possible date falls long after the development of metal-working in Western Asia, raising the possibility that the Chinese may have learned the art from intermediaries who carried it across the continent. However, at present it seems more likely that Chinese metallurgy developed independently, since it possessed important characteristics that were not found elsewhere. Chinese bronze was unusual because it contained lead in addition to the standard copper-tin alloy; and during the early centuries of manufacture Chinese artefacts were made by an elaborate casting method rather than the hammering or 'lost wax' techniques used in other Asian cultures.

The first Chinese bronzes were produced under the Shang dynasty and were elite productions designed for the royal family and nobility. The bronze foundries were established close to the Shang cities, under direct royal control, and their most important manufactures were ritual vessels for use in ceremonies and banquets honouring ancestors. In the course of the Shang period the vessels seem to have lost a little of their sacred quality and to have become status symbols, affirming the possessor's membership of the elite. Shang bronzes are technical as well as artistic masterpieces. The moulds from which they were made consisted of a number of pieces of pottery that fitted tightly together. The surfaces of the moulds were carved with the intricate bands of decoration that would appear on the bronze vessels, which emerged from the kiln needing remarkably little work to finish them off. The vessels are strikingly varied, for example including bird-like spouted tripods and pot-bellied cauldrons. But these and other superbly sculptural forms are far from being imaginative extravagances: they belong to a fixed range of types, named, unvarying in appearance, and fulfilling a designated function. Only a few of the vessels are very large, but they all give an impression of formidable solidity and monumental presence. The relief decoration of squared-off scrolls, whorls and other mysterious shapes is of unknown significance but undoubted, if rather sinister, force. The most famous motif is the taotie, most commonly interpreted as an animal mask or face with bulging eyes and fearsome upper jaw; it appeared earlier (c. 2500 BC) on pieces of jade and, although its significance became forgotten, was employed all through the imperial period thanks to the characteristic Chinese reverence for the past and taste for archaic styles.

Bronzes in the Shang style continued to be made in the Zhou period, but increasingly as status objects. Inlays of materials such as gold, silver and turquoise were favoured, and ornaments and figurines became common; animal subjects were influenced by the art of the nomad peoples with whom the Chinese came into contact. The techniques employed now included 'lost wax' (cire perdue), which basically involved modelling the subject in wax and enclosing it in a mould. When the mould was heated, the wax liquefied and drained away through apertures. Then molten bronze was poured into the mould, filling up the shaped space inside and cooling in the form of the wax model. This enabled craftsmen to produce openwork and similarly delicate and intricate designs that were not possible with the casting technique. During the late Zhou or early Han period, fire-gilding was introduced, endowing bronzes with a golden sheen. As in other arts, everyday subjects were favoured under the Han,

and were treated with a lively realism; well-known items include wrestlers, acrobats and many horses, notably the famous 'flying horse' with one hoof resting on a swallow, found in a 2nd century AD tomb.

Bronze was one of the media in which Buddhist influence on China was strongest, introducing new subjects, poses and groupings that were rapidly adopted and modified by Chinese craftsmen. Unfortunately many Buddhist objects were destroyed during the Tang persecutions and subsequent meltings-down of bronzes, so that what survive are mostly smaller-scale pieces. There were later disasters too, including the loss of the great imperial collection of bronzes when the Song abandoned North China. Song archaizing was in part a threatened culture's response, leading, among other things, to a revival of the 2,000-year-old Shang and Zhou styles. Of later bronzes, easily the most famous were those made under the Ming emperor Xuande (1426–35), which were of such high quality that his reign-title, Xuanzong, was used to describe – and promote – any ware made in roughly similar style.

Shang fantasy and sense of form: wine cooler in the form of a mythical beast; 2nd millennium BC. Other Shang ritual vessels were made as tripods or buckets, always densely ornamented.

SCULPTURE IN STONE AND WOOD

Majestic saviour: colossal Buddha at the great Longmen cave-temple complex; his companions a Bodhisattva and a monk who have survived nearly intact. At Longmen there are hundreds of grottoes and niches, with tens of thousands of Buddhist images.

The Chinese have excelled at carving on a small scale in a number of media, including jade and ivory as well as wood and stone. Their achievement in large-scale sculpture has been more limited, and is mainly associated with the imagery and styles introduced by Buddhism, the Indian religion imported via Central Asia. The Chinese regarded sculpture as skilled craft-work rather than an art, and certainly not on a par with painting and calligraphy. Few Chinese sculptors are even known by name, and none was ranked high in the artistic pantheon.

Although some large-scale stone carving may have been practised earlier, under the Shang, the

examples that survive are relatively small. Apart from fragments of relief carving, they consist of seated human figures and owls, tigers and other animals in marble or limestone. Solid, frontally posed and carved with minimal detail or articulation, they (like Shang bronzes) give an impression of monumentality despite their size. The complex designs engraved on their surfaces are related to those found on contemporary bronzes and reinforce the impression of hieratic remoteness that they convey.

Some wooden ritual objects have been recovered from the kingdom of Chu, one of the leading 'Warring States', whose conquest by Qin was the final step in the creation of the Chinese empire. But the most monumental objects associated with the First Emperor were not of stone or wood but the ceramic army of life-size men and horses that guarded his tomb. Monumental stone sculpture has survived from the Han dynasty in the form of figures of real and fantastic beasts lining the processional way to the tombs. Some tomb walls were decorated with low reliefs which were linear rather than sculptural in character. On the available evidence, there was nothing to suggest that Chinese sculpture would soon take a radical new direction.

Though Buddhism arrived in China during the 1st century AD, it made little impact on the native population until after the collapse of the Han empire ushered in a period of disunity and competing dynasties; in particular, the accession of a Buddhist 'emperor' to the throne of Northern Wei meant that the religion attracted lavish patronage and a large following. Temples and statuary were later destroyed wholesale during the Tang persecutions of Buddhism, but one large group of works in stone survived because of their size and remoteness. These were the spectacular cave-temples which the Chinese constructed in imitation of Indian Buddhist practice, known indirectly from the cave-temples built along the trade and pilgrim routes across Central Asia. Hewn from the living rock of high cliffs, the temples contained hundreds of cells or shrines, and were ornamented with free-standing sculptures and, depending on the quality of the stone, wall-paintings or reliefs. Also following Indian precedent, each cave-complex contained at least one colossal figure of the Buddha, proclaiming the superhuman nature and significance of the Enlightened One.

The earliest cave-temples were excavated at Dunhuang, a settlement on the frontier with Central Asia, in the 4th century; but because of the quality of the stone in the area, it was important for its paintings rather than sculpture. By contrast, the cave-temples at Yungang were entirely decorated with reliefs and free-standing statues, including a 14-metre-high seated Buddha carved in a style derived from Indian or Afghan colossi. Originally flanked by

Bodhisattvas, the figure is broad and solid, but far removed from Han naturalism, its face a smiling mask, its earlobes elongated to suggest pendants, and its draperies schematized.

Yungang was close to the Northern Wei capital of Datong. The importance of royal patronage is suggested by the fact that in 494, when the dynasty moved to a new capital at Luoyang, excavations of cave-temples were begun almost immediately at nearby Longmen. Here, against intricate, all-over relief patterns, the 17-metre-high Buddha and other figures show the partial domestication of Buddhist art in the softening and humanizing of the features and the Chinese taste for delicate, linear, patterned elements even on three-dimensional objects.

A relatively small number of 7th- to 9th-century stone sculptures survived the Tang persecutions, all the more unfortunately in that they are characteristically powerful and imbued with a sense of movement. As the vitality of Buddhism declined, so did the tradition of stone-carving; probably the most interesting works from later periods of Chinese history are the real and fantastic creatures that line the Sacred Way to the Ming imperial tombs outside Beijing.

Left: figures and reliefs in a grotto at Yungang, where cave-temples were carved from the cliffs between 460 and 494. Indian influence is still strong here, by contrast with the softer style that subsequently predominated at Longmen (opposite).

Below: wooden figure of a Daoist deity, made during the Song period. The delicacy of the carving and the elongation of the figure create an effect of mildness and charm, not unlike that of sculptures made for some Gothic cathedrals in Europe.

Made for travelling in style:
lacquered coffer, 1613.
Lacquerworking was intensely
laborious, and despite its sturdy
air this fantastically decorated
piece is clearly a luxury object.

LACQUER AND JADE

Some works of art can only be created with a substantial investment of labour and great technical expertise; so we should expect them to have been made from their beginning for the luxury market of a relatively advanced and sophisticated society. Surprisingly, this was far from the case with two celebrated and highly distinctive products of Chinese civilization: objects of lacquer and jade were being fashioned as early as the Neolithic period, before the Chinese had begun to make use of metals.

The discovery of lacquer is certainly the more remarkable. The substance consists of the sap of the lacquer tree, which at that time grew in China and was obtained like rubber, by tapping. After suitable treatment (mainly drying) it could be coloured with pigments (most commonly red or black) and used like a paint or varnish to coat wood, hemp cloth or other materials. Its functional value lay in the fact that it was heat- and waterproof, enabling it to be used to protect kitchenware and furniture. But it was also decorative, its shiny, colourful surfaces giving distinction to boxes, cups, shoes, military equipment, coffins and many other items; moreover designs could be painted in lacquer on to the lacquer ground that covered an object. By the Han era lacquer-working was an important industrial art, and production-line techniques prevailed in state factories, where half-a-dozen or more specialist tasks were carried out by different craftsmen; one cup is actually inscribed with a list of the craftsmen and officials involved.

More spectacular results could be achieved by multiplying the number of coats and inlaying or carving into the lacquer. These techniques, increasingly popular under the later dynasties, involved an astonishing amount of time and labour. Each coat had to be left to dry for several days before a fresh coat could be applied; and an ambitious project might require up to two hundred coats. Red remained the most-favoured colour, but black, green, gold and yellow were also used; and by the Ming period virtuoso effects were being achieved by applying layers in different colours and cutting designs into them at various depths. An alternative technique was to inlay the lacquer with a different-coloured lacquer or some other material; the most common, creating a brilliant surface effect, was mother-of-pearl.

Fine lacquerwork was valued highly, but nothing was more precious to the Chinese than jade, which was endowed with seemingly magical qualities. Though not (as they believed) indestructible, it is so hard that even steel tools cannot carve it. It is translucent, enticingly smooth and strangely ice-cold to the touch, emits a musical note when struck, and takes a high, oily polish.

Despite their reverence for this mysterious material, the Chinese discovered that it could be shaped – painfully slowly – by using quartzite or other abrasive powders in conjunction with rubbing or boring implements. Jade objects dating from about 3500 BC have been found in the far north-east (Liaoning province) and, in spectacularly large numbers, at a Neolithic site in the Yangtze delta (Liangzhu culture, c. 3300–2200 BC); in both cases the high standard of execution suggests that they were preceded by a long working tradition. Among them were objects that would continue to be fashioned for thousands of years, notably the bi, a flat ring with a circular central aperture, and a faceted rectangular-section tube, the cong; they may already have possessed something like their later significance, symbolic of heaven and earth respectively.

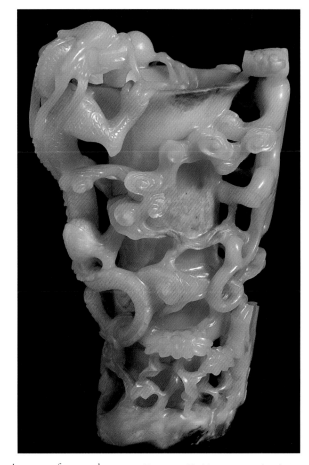

Dragons climbing among clouds to reach the Sacred Pearl of Wisdom. The complexity of the external carving almost conceals the fact that this jade object is a vase or pot; 13th-15th century.

Jade is not in fact a single type of stone, but describes a family with similar properties. The kind most commonly used by the Chinese was nephrite; it was usually green, but might also be brown, buff or white (the colour most prized by the Chinese). Most surprising of all is the fact that jade is not found in China proper, but was being imported even in Neolithic times, almost certainly from distant Xinjiang. Like other materials, it is known primarily in the form of offerings to the dead during and after the Shang period, becoming a luxury secular art under the late Zhou. Increasingly valued by the literati for its aesthetic appeal, it was used to make a wide range of everyday objects from jewellery to chopsticks. Dating of pieces, always difficult, is further complicated by the Song penchant for reviving older styles. After a period of relative neglect when jade was in short supply, the craft underwent a revival under the Qing, who were able to import quantities of jadeite (a material similar to nephrite but glassier) from Burma. Figure and landscape subjects were fashioned, sometimes on extremely large pieces, with immense, if showy, skill.

SILKEN SPLENDOUR

Multi-coloured silk embroidery on white satin. The delicate naturalism and muted colours of the embroidery gives this mid-19th-century fabric a pleasantly spring-like atmosphere.

The most beautiful and luxurious of all fabrics, silk was for centuries China's most precious secret. Neighbouring states sought to acquire it by trade, even at the cost of accepting tributary status, and warlike nomads allowed themselves to be pacified by gifts of the unique, mysteriously soft, smooth, light, lustrous material. Although other commodities were carried into Central Asia from the Han period, it was no accident that the caravan trails came to be known as the Silk Road; and after the fabric reached Rome in the 1st century BC, the fabulous country that lay somewhere at the other end of the trails was given the name Serica, Land of Silk.

According to legend, knowledge of silk-making was brought to China by the mythical empress Xi Ling Shi in about 2500 BC, and there is evidence to suggest that the date is not too far wrong. Traces found in Shang tombs indicate that craftsmen were already producing single-colour fabrics with woven-in designs (damasks) as well as embroideries. Zhou tombs have yielded brocades and gauzes, and under the Han multicoloured silks were produced in quantities for both internal and export markets. The importance of silk is indicated by its prominence in the government's policy of holding reserves of consumer goods to meet possible shortages: no less than five million rolls were stowed away, suggesting that any interruption in supply would have been regarded as a national emergency.

Centuries passed before the outside world learned the secrets of sericulture. The Chinese are reputed to have jealously guarded their knowledge, and entertaining anecdotes explain its eventual spread; silkworm eggs are said to have reached 6th-century Byzantium in the hollow bamboo staffs carried by Persian monks working for the Emperor Justinian. In reality the secretiveness of the entire Chinese population is a less likely explanation than the difficulty of transporting the eggs over long distances and the highly specific conditions which had to be created to achieve successful production. The principal source of silk was the larva of the domestic silk moth, which had to be fed quantities of mulberry leaves for several weeks after hatching. At this point it would spend a few days spinning a cocoon which consisted of something like a thousand metres of silk thread that hardened on exposure to the air. Timing was important in securing the largest possible quantity. Before the pupa matured into a moth and left the cocoon (fouling the threads as it did so), it had to be killed by being placed in boiling water. This also made it easier to wind off the strands, which were then prepared for dyeing and weaving.

Production was on a large scale, and the processes involved were laborious, requiring constant attention to the voracious worms and the maintenance of uniform conditions. Thousands of cocoons were needed to produce a single kilo of silk, but the fabric was so valuable that it was worth the effort; indeed, during periods when there was no central authority – in late Zhou times and again after the collapse of the Han empire – bolts of silk became the only universally acceptable form of currency. Hallowed texts were inscribed on pieces of silk and court paintings were executed on them. Rather more common was the use of brilliantly coloured and decorated silks on such items as banners and canopies; and above all silk was the material in which the emperor and the ruling elite, men and women alike, clothed themselves. Silken garments were such a badge of status that only members of the

governing class were legally allowed to wear them. This decree excluded all merchants, however wealthy, although the fact that they were able to buy and sell the forbidden fabric made it certain that they would disobey. At times when the law was being enforced they could at least enjoy the secret pleasure of wearing silken undergarments, and under the later dynasties wealth could be given respectability by translating it into land or office, allowing its possessors the luxury of flaunting silks in perfect safety.

Ceremonial silk: the official summer robe of one of the court eunuchs who served the late 19th-century Empress Dowager Cixi. It carries a highly visible badge of rank, an imperial dragon, embroidered on the chest.

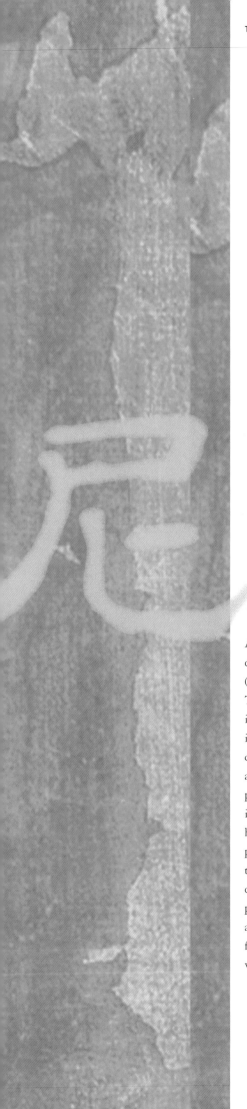

POTTERY AND PORCELAIN

All ceramic wares are essentially objects made of clay that have been shaped and then baked ('fired') in a kiln to achieve the required hardness. The higher the temperature at which the material is fired, the harder, and therefore the less porous, it will be. In the West, this is the basis for the division of wares into progressively higher-fired and harder types: earthenware, stoneware and porcelain. Porcelain, not only hard but astonishingly white, smooth and translucent, has been hailed as the supreme Chinese discovery, and porcelain vessels and figures made by Chinese factories astonished and delighted outsiders. For centuries only the Chinese knew how to make porcelain: the Japanese finally learned the secret after 1500, and Europeans discovered the process for themselves after 1700. Unsurprisingly, the world at large has tended to regard the ceramic

tradition of China as its greatest contribution to the arts. The tradition began at a remarkably early date. Even in prehistoric times the distinctively Chinese feeling for harmonious relationships between form and decoration was asserting itself. By the 3rd millennium BC, pottery of the Yangshao culture in North China was being painted with elegant swirling or geometric designs, beautifully integrated with the forms of the vessels. But equally striking in their own way are the wares of the north-eastern Longshan culture, undecorated, black and burnished; some are made in remarkable shapes, as tall ringed beakers and jugs with spouts, sectioned and studded and resting on tripod legs. More like sculptures than ceramic vessels, these might be taken for imitation bronzes had bronze-working existed in China at this time: instead, the affinity of the pots with the very much later bronzes of the Shang period suggests that the influence was exerted in the opposite direction, bridging the Neolithic and Bronze Ages.

Humbler wares, decorated by some form of stamping or incision, also maintained the same recognizable character as the Chinese made the transition to a dynastic and literate culture. Most of the evidence for the Shang, Zhou and Han periods comes from burials, and the pottery objects found in them not only resembled contemporary bronzes but were probably intended to serve as cheap substitutes for the metal. During the Warring States period (464–222 BC) beautiful, elaborate ceramic tiles began to be made, and eventually they replaced thatch on the houses of the wealthy. Under the Han, the main technical innovation was the introduction of the first true glazes during the 2nd century BC. A glaze is a coating of glass applied to a clay body which makes it impervious to liquids, a particularly useful function in view of the porousness of earthenware; nevertheless it has been suggested that this first, green glaze was widely used because it created a surface effect that resembled the patina of old bronzes.

The commonest Han wares were wine jars, but the most interesting vessels to the lay person are the incense burners known as 'hill jars'. Mounted on three small feet, these were equipped with a cone-shaped lid moulded to represent the Daoist Isles of the Blessed, in the form of a mountain-island surrounded by waves; a moulded frieze decorated with dragon, tiger and bird forms often encircled the body.

When human beings were no longer sacrificed to furnish the dead person with concubines, servants and guards, pottery figures provided substitutes. As we have seen, the tombs of the Qing and Han emperors were protected at a distance by earthenware armies which involved casting on a large scale as well as the individual modelling of facial features. The imperial tombs have not been excavated, but the contents of Han tombs have been a prime source of information about the everyday life of the period, largely thanks to the number of pottery models that have been unearthed. In his comfortable afterlife a Han gen-

tleman might find himself surrounded by members of his family, protected by fearsome, martial tomb guardians, entertained by acrobats and musicians, and able to survey farm buildings and animals, pigsty, well and watchtower, perhaps from the seat of an earthenware horse belonging to the recently imported 'blood-sweating' breed from Ferghana.

Like other Han wares, these funerary models were either glazed or painted directly on to an already-fired body covered with white or red slip. (Slip is potter's clay diluted to a creamy consistency and used variously as a ground, as trailed decoration, or as a cement with which to join on separate pieces of pottery.) The models continued to be made during the period of disunity that followed, but most were painted on to unglazed surfaces. They anticipate some features of Tang tomb pottery, which is, however, incomparably more realistic, forceful and lively. This now world-famous art was never intended to be seen by mortal eyes, and was virtually unknown until the early years of the 20th century, when the construction of a railway line disturbed a number of

Opposite: painted earthenware jar from the Yangshao culture (c.4000–3000 BC), the earliest Neolithic culture in the Yellow River valley. Made without a wheel, such pieces exhibit remarkable potting and decorative skills.

Below: pottery model of a palace gate, found in a Han dynasty tomb. During this period, pottery was widely used for miniaturized imitations of real objects, designed to accompany the dead person into the afterlife.

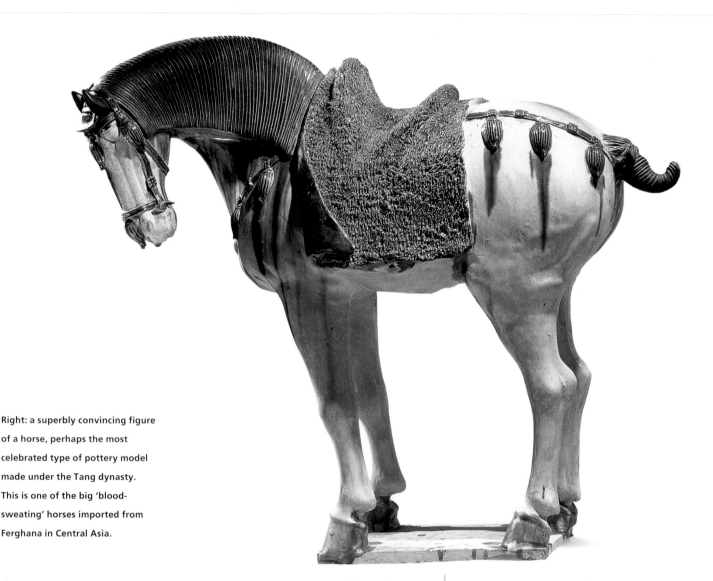

Right: a superbly convincing figure of a horse, perhaps the most celebrated type of pottery model made under the Tang dynasty. This is one of the big 'blood-sweating' horses imported from Ferghana in Central Asia.

Opposite: vase with dragon-headed handles. Pottery of this type is reminiscent of Greek amphoras and does in fact display non-Chinese influences; this is quite characteristic of the Tang period's cosmopolitan culture.

tombs. Subsequent excavations revealed that the figures were made in very large numbers, reflecting the wealth and power of Tang China.

The most celebrated Tang figures are horses and camels, strongly modelled and with an unmistakable inner life and sense of momentarily interrupted movement. But the figures of oxen, birds and other animals, attendants, musicians, dancers, beggars, wrestlers, and extra-large tomb guardians have an equally impressive physical presence. As if designed to illustrate the cosmopolitan spirit of the era, the figures also include representations of foreigners (some of them clearly intended as caricatures) including mounted Central Asians, widely employed as retainers at Changan. Most of the figures were cast from moulds, and the larger examples were made in sections and assembled. Some are unglazed and painted, but the majority are deco-

rated with a wider range of coloured glazes (green, brown, yellow, cream, black, even difficult-to-achieve blue) developed under the Tang; they have sometimes been splashed on and have usually been allowed to run, creating an interestingly irregular or mottled effect.

Pottery vessels and dishes of distinction were also made during the period. Some types were strongly influenced by foreign contacts, notably vases with dragon handles, slender necks and large bellies, reminiscent of Greek amphoras, and horned drinking-cups, or rhytons, based on Western Asian vessels. After the Tang period, however, the earthenware tradition was to be eclipsed by the development of harder materials, namely stoneware and porcelain.

Westerners divide ceramics into three types, distinguishing not only earthenware but stoneware from porcelain, on the grounds that porcelain alone is white and translucent. By contrast, the Chinese consider stoneware and porcelain as a single group, based on the fact that both will give out a ringing tone when lightly tapped. There is a good deal to be said for the Chinese view, which dispenses with awkward terms such as 'proto-porcellanous' to describe betwixt-and-between wares; and it is not open to the logical objection that porcelain, however fine, is only translucent when thinly potted, quite apart from the fact that its whiteness is only significant on pieces which have not been covered with coloured glazes. In China, both stoneware and porcelain were fired at about the same temperature (some 1,300 degrees C by comparison with the 800 degrees C which sufficed for earthenware), and both were covered with a glaze made from feldspathic rock (which became vitreous only when fired at very high temperatures), rather than with the glassy substance used for earthenware. However, whereas the body colour of stoneware varies from black to light grey, porcelain is white, thanks to its unique ingredients: a very pure white china clay, called kaolin, which was mixed with a feldspathic rock known by the Franco-Chinese term petuntse (the material that was also used for the glaze); the vitrification of the petuntse during firing was responsible for the hardness and smoothness of the porcelain.

The manufacture of a higher-fired material than earthenware – in effect, a type of stoneware – has been traced back in China as far as the Zhou period. A more sustained tradition was initiated under the Han, and by the Tang period the best-known ware, from Yue in the province of Shanxi, already had a long history behind it; Yue vases and bowls of this period are typically carved with mythological and floral designs and covered with an olive-green glaze.

It was also under the Tang dynasty that the earliest examples of porcelain were made, although little of this ware now survives. At least one visitor from the Near East, a certain Suleyman, was struck by the very quality that later impressed Europeans; in 851 he observed that 'the Chinese have a fine clay from which they make vessels equal in quality to glass, for you can see the liquid they hold inside them.'

The Song era has generally been regarded as the pinnacle of Chinese ceramic artistry. This was not achieved by colourful decoration or obvious virtuosity: most Song forms are simple, decorated with restrained carved or moulded designs, and covered with a single-colour glaze. Their supreme appeal lies in their harmonious proportions and the perfectly judged relationship between form and decoration; it has been said that an ardent collector who spent a lifetime in studying Chinese ceramics would ultimately die in possession of a single, simple, undecorated Song bowl!

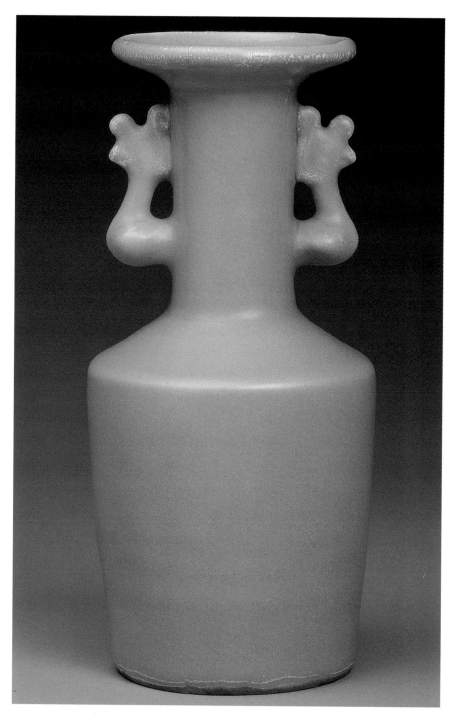

Above: a mallet vase, a form also known by the Japanese term Kinuta. This one is Longchuan celadon ware with its typically very thick glaze; Southern Song dynasty.

the Northern Song in 1127. The Guan ('official') ware of the Southern Song had a dark body which showed through the glaze at the rim and base, causing the Chinese to label it 'brown mouth and iron foot'. Stoneware made at Cizhou was decorated by the sgraffito (Italian, 'scratched') technique, which involved covering the grey body with white slip and then cutting through to the ground to create a two-tone design. Quieter but no less pleasing effects were achieved by the Northern and Southern Celadons, stonewares with grey, green or blue-green glazes; clearly derived from the Yue ware tradition, they are among the great formal masterpieces of Song ceramics. Finally, it was under the Song that Jingdezhen, near Nanjing, became a major centre of porcelain production, initially thanks to the singularly pure clay found in the area. It was the most important, though not the sole, producer of a type of ware known as Qingbai ('bluish white') or Yingqing ('shadowy blue'), in reference to the faint blue-green tinge of the white glaze.

Jingdezhen continued to operate under the Mongol Yuan dynasty, producing an official

From this point, the history of Chinese ceramics is known in considerable detail, and only a few wares and the most important technical and artistic developments can be noted here. The industry flourished under the Song, and many types are referred to by site names such as Jun (stoneware with a lavender glaze sometimes splashed with red or purple). Some wares were made exclusively for the imperial court, notably Ding white porcelain and the rare, grey-green Ju, produced only during the twenty years before the overthrow of

Left: unusually restrained for its period, this Ming porcelain jar is undecorated except for its brilliant yellow enamel overglaze. Late 16th century.

Opposite: large Yungqing vase with incised decoration. Under the Song this ware (also known as Qingbai) was manufactured and exported in large quantities.

white-glazed ware known as Shufu because the decorations often included the Chinese characters shu and fu, trailed on to the body with slip. During the Yuan period the decorative repertoire used on stoneware and porcelain was enlarged by the discovery of pigments that could withstand the temperatures needed to fuse glazes. Previously, painting could only be done with 'cold' pigments, on to the glaze or a body that was to be left unglazed. But blue pigment, derived from cobalt oxide imported from Persia, could be painted on to the surface of an already-fired pot, which could then be glazed and fired again without spoiling the decoration; the result was 'blue and white', one of the most widely known of all ceramic wares. Able to work with much greater freedom, decorators employed fluent brushwork to create designs with birds, flowers, fish, plants, dragons and phoenixes that were often crowded and intricate but very skilfully balanced. Underglaze painting was also done with a copper red, although the results were much less certain.

Ceramic production was affected relatively little by the upheavals that drove out the Mongols.

Under the new Ming dynasty the kilns at Jingdezhen grew into a vast industrial complex. Porcelain was now indisputably the most prestigious material for ceramics, and there was a huge demand for wares of varying qualities and prices. At the same time Ming taste swung away from Song restraint towards more assertive shapes and enhanced decorative appeal. In combination, these trends encouraged a more mass-production system at Jingdezhen, where potters and decorators took on specialized roles.

However, there was no falling off in quality. In fact blue-and-white ware was made to higher technical standards and became more refined, remaining so throughout the period, despite difficulties caused by the exhaustion of cobalt sup-

plies and the rather different effects created by its replacement. Among the many fine examples are unusual pieces made for high-ranking Muslims, which carry inscriptions in Arabic.

Other kilns were opened or expanded their operations in the South, partly in response to the growing demand from abroad. Dehua produced small, finely modelled porcelain figures covered with a lustrous white glaze; representations of the Buddhist goddess Guanyin are especially appealing, but other deities and sages, animals, and small objects such as seals for the mandarin's writing table were also made. At its best during the early Qing period (late 17th and early 18th century), this type of ware became known in Europe as blanc de chine, helping to give porcelain figurines a long-lasting vogue in the West.

The Ming taste for decoration and brighter colours led to the introduction of overglaze painting. This was done with pigments, known as enamel colours, which were applied over the glaze or directly on to the fired body (when the enamels in effect served as a glaze), after which the piece was given a secondary firing; as with underglaze colours, this was done at a lower temperature which fixed without destroying the enamels.

Overglaze colours played a much larger role under China's last imperial dynasty, the Qing. Superb blue-and-white (underglaze) ware continued to be made during the reign of Kangxi (1661–1722), but this was increasingly surpassed

Right: porcelain brush pot with famille verte (predominantly green) overglaze decoration. It shows a sage taking tea; Qing ware, made during the reign of Kangxi (1662–1722).

Opposite: Chinese porcelain made for export. The roundel in the centre of the plate, showing a doctor's visit, is based on a European design; famille rose, c.1738.

in popularity by wares painted in several enamel colours and grouped in 'families': famille verte, famille noire, famille jaune and famille rose, each labelled according to the predominant colour in the designs (green, black, yellow, rose-pink). The rose-pink is an interesting example of European influence, probably introduced by Jesuit missionaries and the most popular of all these wares, which were primarily made for export. Chinese porcelain continued to be in great demand until the later 18th century, and serious efforts were made to adapt to the requirements of the European market. Plates with flat rims were produced, along with novelties such as porcelain musical instruments, while decorations sometimes included figures of Europeans and fanciful, 'exotic' motifs. Among the most curious export wares were 'armorial' dinner services carrying the coat of arms of an individual who had thought it worth sending a picture of it to the East for Chinese workmen to put on to porcelain.

Under Kangxi and his successor Yongzheng (1723–35), the kilns at Jingdezhen were run by a series of imperial directors who encouraged technical and artistic innovation. The most remarkable results were glazes that were extraordinary for their colours and visual textures, aptly conveyed by some of their names: peachbloom, teadust, clair de lune (better in the Chinese version, 'moon white') and sang de boeuf (ox-blood).

Letters written in 1712 and 1722 by the Jesuit Père d'Entrecolles describe in detail the operations of the Jingdezhen factories. They make it clear that a very advanced division-of-labour system prevailed, with each worker performing a single small task. When d'Entrecolles was making his observations this had certainly not led to any deterioration in the quality of Jingdezhen wares; but it is possible that mechanical working methods were a factor in the decline that became apparent by the mid-18th century, perhaps furthered by an archaizing tendency that encouraged virtuoso imitation rather than creativity. The artistic falling-off was followed in the troubled 19th century by a lowering of technical standards, so that in ceramics, as in other respects, imperial China appeared to have become moribund even before its final passing.

A pilgrim flask, so called because European pilgrims carried similarly shaped flasks, passing a strap through the lugs at the shoulder; Qing porcelain with blue-and-white decoration.

Right, opposite: Buddhist painting
from the Dunhuang caves. It
shows women making offerings to
Avalokitesvara, the Bodhisattva
later transformed by the Chinese
into the goddess Guanyin; ink and
colours on linen, AD 664.

Right, opposite: Buddhist painting
from the Dunhuang caves. It
shows women making offerings to
Avalokitesvara, the Bodhisattva
later transformed by the Chinese
into the goddess Guanyin; ink and
colours on linen, AD 664.

Right: Lady Feng and the Bear, an
illustration from 'Admonitions of
the Instructress to the Court
Ladies' by Gu Kaizhi. Despite the
lack of any background detail, the
interrelationship between the
figures holds the scene together.

THE ARTS OF THE BRUSH

Nothing is known of painting as an independent activity until the Han period (206 BC–AD 220). The art was already flourishing, as is made clear by references in literary sources to great cycles of wall paintings which illustrated Confucian moral subjects or the rival Daoist world of myth and magic. But none of these prestigious objects have survived. Our knowledge of Han painting, as of other Han arts, comes from the excavation of tombs, and with the exception of a splendid, mysterious, symbol-rich painted banner from the Former Han period, the works that have been recovered from them are decorations on brick walls, boxes and similar objects.

These can hardly be representative of Han painting as a whole, yet they do display some characteristics of Chinese art that are found through much of its history. In particular, fluent, sensitive brushlines define the figures in the best-known Han scene, a painting of a group of officials from a tomb near Luoyang. Their distinctive facial expressions and dance-like attitudes, and the strong sense that they are interacting with one another, create an atmosphere in which it is easy for the viewer to believe that witty or profound remarks are being made. This and a more damaged companion painting are narrative scenes, probably illustrating well-known historical or proverbial episodes.

The Han emperors are known to have been as enthusiastic in accumulating art treasures as any of the later Chinese dynasties. When the capital was sacked during a civil war in AD 190, a boorish soldiery used silk paintings from the imperial collection as materials from which to make tents and knapsacks. A mere seventy cartloads were rescued and transported to safety; half survived a long journey westward, but even these have long since disappeared.

The century and a half following the collapse of the Han empire is virtually a blank in the history of Chinese painting. Court arts evidently flourished among the southern dynasties, but only one artist can be linked to specific works with any confidence. Gu Kaizhi (c. 344–c. 406) worked for the Jin court at Nanjing and is known for two paintings on silk handscrolls, *The Nymph of the Lon River* and *Admonitions of the Instructress to the Court Ladies*. Both, although later copies, are believed to be reasonably faithful to the originals. In fact the copy of the *Admonitions*, itself very old, is the earliest surviving example of scroll painting. It consists of scenes, painted in ink and colour, that serve as illustrations to the columns of text that separate them. These are Confucian moral discourses, and although the commentary embodied in the paintings is not always explicit, an element of psychological tension is very obviously present. Gu Kaizhi himself is said to have been an eccentric personality, Daoist rather than Confucian, and well-known without necessarily being regarded as the greatest artist of his day.

Ironically, systematic art criticism began during this period, surviving far more successfully than the works it discussed. The 6th-century writings of Xie He list six criteria for judging a painting, of which the first and most general is 'vitality achieved through spirit consonance'. This involves the attainment of an intimate vital sympathy between the artist, the subjects pictured and the world at large. Fidelity to appearance comes further down Xie He's list, reflecting a priority – expressiveness rather than literalism – that became the most important of Chinese aesthetic canons.

Like sculpture in stone, paintings from the 5th century onwards only survived in any numbers at Buddhist cave-temple sites. Sculpture was the preferred medium for decorating them, so it was a fortunate accident that the stone at Dunhuang was unsuitable for carving. Dunhuang stood at the western end of the Chinese world, absorbing influences from Central Asia at an early date and becoming a centre of Buddhist settlement. Many times extended, its 'Thousand-Buddha Caves' became renowned, and a wall-painting tradition

The Emperor Ming Huang travelling in Shu; later copy of an 8th-century painting. Despite the presence of human figures and an element of narrative, this is essentially an early example of Chinese landscape art.

was sustained there from the 5th to the 8th centuries. The figures in early frescoes are rather stiff and foursquare, reflecting Central Asian styles, but a more lively and decorative Chinese style soon prevailed. The most popular subjects were jatakas, episodes from the legendary earlier lives of the Buddha; these gave a certain scope to the painter's imagination despite the cramping effect of laying out the subjects in horizontal registers and other devices that framed and broke up the composition. These were being dispensed with by the late 7th century, and large-scale compositions were created that took advantage of the vast spaces available. Appropriately ambitious subjects were chosen from stories about Buddhas and Bodhisattvas, but even more striking were representations of the Western Paradise, the reward promised to true believers by the popular Pure Land version of the faith; here, painters could work on the grand scale, creating flower-decked palaces, halls and temples where musicians, dancers and celebrants disported themselves under the benevolent gaze of the Buddha Amitabha. Dunhuang also yielded thousands of manuscripts (including the famous printed Diamond Sutra) and many paintings on silk, stored in a sealed cave-library and forgotten until they were discovered by a Daoist monk in about 1899 and carried off a few years later, in cavalier acts of cultural imperialism, by British and French archaeologists.

The wall paintings at Dunhuang were certainly not the finest examples produced under the Tang, but their remoteness enabled them to

Two Horses and a Groom, a painting by the 8th-century artist Han Gan, who was renowned for his studies of horses. Among the inscriptions on the painting is that of the Song emperor Huizong, dating from 1107.

survive periods of persecution and other political upheavals that destroyed some of the greatest of all Chinese works. At any rate that seems the only conclusion that can be drawn from accounts of Wu Daozi (c. 700–760), an artist who has been described as the Michelangelo of China because of the frenzied energy with which he painted hundreds of frescoes on Buddhist subjects as well as creating works in other genres; not a single example of his art survives. The destruction cannot be attributed solely to religious persecution, since Tang secular painting fared even worse: the most important extant examples are some fine dignified wall paintings from the tombs of Princess Yong Tai and other high-ranking personages near the capital, Changan, and a painted silk scroll with imaginary portraits of thirteen emperors, attributed to Yan Liben (d. 673), but perhaps

painted rather later. In both instances the figures are drawn in a large, bold style that is unusual in Chinese painting but characteristic of Tang attitudes in all the arts; the best-known image among the Thirteen Emperors, of the Han sovereign Wudi, has an extraordinary presence which suggests that it may be the portrait of a real person, albeit not the long-dead emperor. This is also true of the single, partly restored painting which is the only surviving work attributed to Han Gan, the most famous of all Tang horse painters.

Scholars of the Northern Qi Collating the Classic Texts is a fine, appropriately busy painting that has been attributed to Yan Liben although, as is so often the case, the surviving copy is of a later date. Informal glimpses of Chinese life are all too rare, but two charming scenes, *Ladies Playing Double Sixes* and *Tuning the Lute and Drinking Tea* are attributed to the Tang painter Zhou Fang (working c. 780–810). Fortunately the figure-painting impulse carried over into the Five Dynasties and early Song periods. At one of the Five Dynasties courts, that of the Southern Tang, Gu Hongzhong painted *Night Entertainment of Han Xicai*, a series of scenes on a silk handscroll which shows Han and his friends experiencing the delights of wine, women and song. The scroll is said to have been painted on the orders of the Southern Tang sovereign, who was inclined to promote Han to high office but was worried by his reputation for debauchery; so Gu Hongzhong was deputed to join in the revels and report back in pictorial as well as verbal form. Disorder of a different kind appears in Zhou Wenju's *Ladies Bathing Children* and in a few 11th- and 12th-century crowd scenes such as *Lady Wen Ji's Captivity in Mongolia and her Return to China*, Zhang Zeduan's sprightly account of life *Along the River at the Time of the Qingming Festival* and Zhao Bozhu's *Palaces of Han*.

Among the lost arts of the Tang was landscape painting, which subsequently became by far the most important kind of Chinese painting. Although landscapes had figured prominently in some earlier works, it seems to have been under the Tang that they began to be represented for their own sakes, rather than as the settings for religious or moral episodes. It was also during this

period that some innovators began to paint in monochrome, using only black calligraphic ink applied with a brush; they may originally have chosen this austere medium as a fastidious reaction against the bright colours and bustling paradises of popular Buddhist art. Traditionally attributed to the 8th-century poet and painter Wang Wei, the black-and-white 'poem without words' later became identified with the artistic self-expression of cultivated amateurs – the literati or scholar-officials, who practised it when at leisure from their duties or living in retirement. By contrast, colour continued to be employed by the professional artists working for the imperial court or wealthy patrons, whose taste ran to works such as large-scale decorative schemes. This 'blue and green' art came to be despised by the literati (not always justly) as commercial hackwork; Chinese art history generally endorsed their point of view and exalted the literati landscape as the supreme form of painting – perhaps reflecting the fact that members of the literati class wrote the histories.

The very high place held by landscape painting seems surprising to westerners, whose own art has tended to be emphatically human-centred. Significantly, the Chinese developed an intense feeling for the natural world at a very early date (in the West, the same feeling is little more than two hundred years old), most strikingly embodied

Studies of a sheep and a goat; ink on paper, mounted on silk. The artist, Zhao Mengfu (1254–1322), spent most of his life under the alien Yuan dynasty, and was later much criticized for serving them.

in the Daoist cult of mountains and streams, and the Daoist sense of a cosmic force flowing through all things. Inspired by just such a sense, the Chinese landscapist could never become a pure observer and recorder. Though he studied nature closely, he painted scenes that did not represent real places; but these were not so much imaginary as imbued with the vital, essential qualities of a landscape. And, as we have seen, for the artist himself, 'vitality achieved through spirit consonance' was even more important than technical accomplishments.

In this scheme of things human beings were part of nature, and only a small part at that; so it is not surprising to find that they usually appeared in landscape paintings as minuscule figures whose activities had no special significance. At the same time, the subjects represented were restricted to the natural world; as if to repudiate Buddhist miracle and Daoist magic, the artist excluded from his work all supernatural elements and fabulous beasts. It is one of the paradoxes of Chinese art that the supreme form of self-expression should have been one in which the human element played at best a subsidiary role, and that generations of painters should have developed highly personal styles while manipulating the same very restricted repertoire of motifs: rocks, plants, mist, a stream or waterfall, a bridge, a hut or pagodas.

The landscapists also confined themselves to the simplest technical means. Some painters added a few touches of colour to their compositions, but generally speaking these were executed in monochrome. The implements were a brush, made with animal hair, fitted into a bamboo holder, and ink which came in the form of a stick of lamp-black, dissolved before use by being rubbed against a moistened stone. The ink was intensely black, but could be diluted and applied in various shades of grey.

The brush and ink used for painting were identical with those employed by the literati in writing – and not by accident, since both activities were part of a visual aesthetic. With their taste for nuances, the Chinese tended to rate calligraphy even more highly as an art than painting. The flexible brush was capable of laying on a range of thick or thin strokes, and connoisseurs picked out differences in nervous energy and pressure, scrutinized the relationships between the components of an individual character, and examined critically the arrangement of the characters on a page. From at least the 4th century AD famous calligraphers were developing classic handwriting styles, and the Tang emperor Taizong is said to have chosen his ministers largely on the basis of their skills as calligraphers.

The same tools and the same controlled movements were used in calligraphy and painting, so many artists became masters of both; and under the Song the development of individual handwriting styles, each designed to express its author's personality, was linked with a comparable

A 10th-century painting from Dunhuang, showing the Indian prince Siddhartha and his groom riding. The prince's experiences led him to reject the world and become the great religious teacher known as the Buddha.

impulse towards self-expression in painting. From Yuan times the ultimate link was forged when landscape paintings began to be accompanied by poems whose sentiments were appropriate to the scene, executed in a fine calligraphy that harmonized visually with the painting to create a satisfyingly complete experience. In this way painting, calligraphy and poetry – the three main leisure pursuits of the literati – could be combined in a single work of art.

The format of paintings was also an important element in the Chinese aesthetic. For centuries they were executed on silk, commonly in the form of hangings or handscrolls – that is, elongated vertical or horizontal shapes which lent themselves to detailed scrutiny rather than the absorption of an overall impression. In fact the handscroll could only be viewed in sections, since it was held in two hands and unrolled horizontally by the spectator, who 'read' it bit by bit from right to left, keeping roughly the same length of scroll open to view. Consequently Chinese landscapes are not uniform compositions in the western sense, but unfold over time and space,

Dwelling in the Fuchun Mountains, 1350, by Huang Gongwang. Huang was one of several late Yuan masters who, finding no employment under the Mongol dynasty, devoted themselves to landscape painting.

Imperial art: birds and lichi, from a handscroll painted by Huizong, the last Northern Song emperor; ink and colours on silk. Huizong founded an Academy of Painting which held examinations and laid down standards.

inviting the eye to enter and make a journey through changing scenery. The artist may predetermine the route by sharply detailing some features while leaving others generalized or misty, and transitions may be smooth or abrupt, depending on the painter's style or the effect to be achieved. It is almost needless to add that the reproduction of landscape details in art books gives only a partial idea of the experience which the Chinese scroll painting could offer.

An alternative format was the album leaf, intended to form part of a set of leaves linked in concertina fashion and enclosed within wooden boards to form a book. This became important late in the Northern Song period, when the

throne was occupied by Huizong, effectively the last emperor to reign from Kaifeng (1101–25). The emperor, a gifted painter and calligrapher, specialized in the already well-established genre of bird- and flower-paintings in the album format, a taste which imperial patronage no doubt helped to spread; exquisitely coloured and deceptively simple in design, pictures in this genre represent the decorative tradition at its best. Huizong was also a compulsive collector and evidently certain of the rightness of his own taste. He founded an Academy of Painting in which examinations were held to select the best artists and the winners were rewarded with official posts. Academies have often been accused of stultifying the arts by attempting to direct their activities, and Huizong was reputedly a difficult taskmaster, but there is no doubt that Song painting flourished. Even the destruction of the Northern Song did not stifle it, although the transfer of the capital and the leading artists to Hangzhou visibly affected landscape painting by replacing rugged northern views with softer, mistier, southern-based scenes which encouraged the use of ink washes and other 'impressionistic' brush techniques; often the result was to create an atmosphere that can only be described as romantic. The distinction between court and literati painters was still far from absolute, and some of the most evocative Southern Song land-

Exquisite blossoms, painted in deceptively simple 'boneless' style (without outlines) and accompanied by a poem which forms part of the overall design; ink and colour on paper, from an album of fruit and flowers.

scapes were the work of artists attached to the court such as Ma Yuan (died 1225) and Xia Gui (died 1230).

One thing that did set the literati artists apart was their increasing preference for painting on paper, which proved more amenable to a variety of textural effects than did silk. Self-expression had begun to play a larger part in landscape, a tendency taken to its extreme in painters associated with the Chan (Zen) school of Buddhism. The central feature of Chan was the moment of individual enlightenment, often achieved through a shock that rent the veil of illusion and induced a sense of oneness with creation. The Chan painter attempted to express such a necessarily brief moment through spontaneous, violent, cursory brushwork which might distort visible reality, but reached deep into the heart of nature. Classics of the Chan style include Liang Kai's imaginary portrait of the Tang poet Li Bo and the celebrated group of persimmons created by Mu Qi with a few patches of ink and strokes of the pen. Interestingly, Chan painting has always been too violent for Chinese taste, though it has been widely admired elsewhere.

Following the Yuan conquest of China, the separateness of the literati painters became more marked, since most of them were unwilling or unable to take up an official career under the alien dynasty; Qian Xuan 'clenched his teeth and did not join the crowd', while Ni Zan, having lost all his wealth, went to live in a houseboat rather than come to terms with the regime. Even the brilliant Zhao Mengfu, never quite forgiven by Chinese historians for accepting a civil service post under the Mongols, retired early in order to paint as he pleased. These and like-minded painters developed subtle, individual styles in which they reinterpreted the great works of the past, combining nostalgia with self-expression in a highly distinctive fashion; their art was intended for a tiny elite-of-the-elite, often little more than the circle of intimate friends among whom their scrolls would be handed round. Some forms of painting contained coded messages of resistance to the Mongols; commonly employed symbols were the bamboo, which bends but does not break, signifying adaptation without loss of integrity, and the plum blossom, which appears in cold weather, like the culture nurtured by scholars during the Mongol Ice Age.

From 1368 China was again ruled by a native dynasty, the Ming. But the first Ming emperor was no friend to the literati, and many who could afford to do so remained in retirement, for preference in the warm South. The integration of calligraphy, painting and poetry that took place in this period might be taken as symbolic of a completely aesthetic view of life. Among the outstanding masters were Shen Zhou (1427–1509) and his pupil Wen Zhengmin (1470–1559). Wen's history suggests that not all literati painters were high-mindedly independent, since he is known to have been a late starter as an artist, having failed the official civil service examinations no less than twenty-eight times. Nevertheless he became a great innovator, producing very fine interpretations of classic paintings and employing bold notes of colour. Other artists, notably Qiu Ying (c. 1494–c. 1552), were even more eclectic, and painting during the Ming and Qing periods embraced a great diversity of styles and schools. The experimentalism of painters such as Wen was answered towards the end of the Ming period by the emergence of a consciously 'Orthodox School' based on the work of the Song and Yuan literati; but that was challenged in turn by the 'Individualists' and the 'Yangzhou Eccentrics'. Nothing better demonstrates the inexhaustibility of art than the variety of doctrines and interpretations that were generated by Chinese painting, despite the self-limited stock of subjects and technical means at the disposal of its practitioners. The only serious deviation from fundamentals took place in the 18th century, when Lang Shining (1688–1766), actually an Italian Jesuit named Giuseppe Castiglione, created a hybrid Western-Chinese style, incorporating elements of perspective and chiaroscuro (light and shadow), which pleased the Emperor Qianlong and inspired some imitators. By the 19th century, western pressure was felt in many areas of life and resented, encouraging painters to adhere rigidly to established styles, so that the imperial era did end in what appeared to be creative exhaustion.

BUILDING IN STYLE

Bright paint and shining tiles, upturned eaves and multiple, ornamented roofs: the traditional architecture of China creates a delightfully exotic impression that makes it easy to overlook the fundamental simplicity of its layout and construction. Whether they were intended as modest houses or magnificent palaces, dwellings consisted of rectangular hall-like units, built almost entirely of wood. They were constructed on the pillar-and-beam principle – that is, the tops of two pillars, one at the front and one at the rear of the main space, were linked by a sturdy beam. A series of such pillars and beams provided the framework for the walls and the base for the roof structure, which consisted of a kingpost, rising from the centre of each beam to support the ridge line of the pitched roof, plus a more or less complicated set of rafters, purlins and brackets. If the hall was to be not only long but broad, secondary or tertiary sets of pillars might have to be added further forward or back, underneath the slope of the roof. Pillars, doors, windows and other features were laid out according to the principle of symmetry so dear to the Chinese.

The plan of Chinese dwellings was equally straightforward. Each was built in the form of a courtyard, with a main hall in the north from which two smaller, symmetrical wings extended at right-angles to the south; the long inner side of the hall faced the entrance. All Chinese buildings were designed to face due south unless the peculiarities of the site made some modification unavoidable; the positive, yang quality of a southern orientation was such that the main gate of a city was always in that quarter, and if the city was an imperial capital a grand processional way led through the gate to the southern entrance of the palaces, the emperor's inner sanctum being located at the furthest, northernmost point of the complex. Similarly, a well-off family built their mansion in the form of a double court, the first allocated to domestic staff and visitors, while the (northernmost) court at the back was reserved for family use. Building on a grander scale entailed no novelty in the layout, merely a multiplication of courtyards to the back or sides. Dwellings presented blank facades to the outside world, their windows facing inwards on to the court, and, like palaces and cities, they were enclosed by walls.

The principal buildings were raised on platforms and painted in bold colours (red, white, blue and green) with yellow or green tiles; the eaves, and the multiple brackets beneath them were significant decorative features, embellished in the finest examples with roof ornaments. The most imposing traditional buildings to have survived are those in the Forbidden City, the imperial palace complex in Beijing. Surrounded by a moat and a 24-kilometre wall, it was formerly part of the walled 'Imperial City', which itself stood within the walled city proper. The

The Great Goose Pagoda at Xian. Pagodas on the site have a long history dating back to AD 652, when it was part of the Tang capital, Changan. The present seven-storey building was erected under the Qing.

Forbidden City was constructed for the Ming emperor Yongle from 1404, replacing a roughly similar complex built for the Yuan Mongol dynasty and destroyed by Yongle's father, the first Ming emperor Hongwu. Though partly rebuilt by the Qing, the Forbidden City is much the same as it was in Yongle's time, a huge rectangle within which palaces, halls, secretarial and household offices, storehouses, servants' and eunuchs' quarters, an archery ground and gardens are neatly laid out on either side of the processional avenue and ramp leading northward to the Dragon Pavement, itself the preliminary to a series of solemn halls and the inner court and imperial residences. The artificial River of Golden Water, meandering across the southern end of the compound, is the only feature that strikes an irregular, picturesque note.

Ironically, the architectural form that most people think of as typically Chinese originated as an import from India. The pagoda was a version of the Buddhist stupa, a shrine created to house religious relics; it was 'naturalized' by being provided, in Chinese fashion, with several storeys (on occasion as many as thirteen), each with its own separate roof. Unlike most Chinese buildings, these towers have been constructed in a number of forms and with a variety of materials; in fact the oldest surviving Chinese building, dating from AD 523, is a pagoda made of brick.

The Forbidden City, Beijing, in 1980; a print (aquatint and etching) by Patrick Procktor, a modern western artist. With its cleverly chosen viewpoint, it captures the rather bleak grandeur of the imperial residences.

Homage to China's most famous poet: an imaginary portrait of Li Bo, painted in the 18th century. Like many traditional images of the sort, it gives no hint of Li Bo's unconventional and sometimes wayward lifestyle.

THE LITERARY TRADITION

Some Neolithic pottery found in China carries designs that may (or may not) be written characters. But the earliest certain examples of a script, recognizably the ancestor of the modern Chinese language, are the questions and answers scratched on to oracle bones late in the Shang period (c. 1750–1027 BC). Its association with religious ritual may be a reason why the written word came to be regarded with such reverence, and why those who possessed the art of writing – the scholar-officials or literati – secured recognition as a cultural and political elite. Reverence for writing is also, inevitably, reverence for the attitudes and doctrines of the past, as preserved in books, and this perhaps explains the conservatism of traditional China, in which originality was not prized or praised, and change, when it did occur, was generally presented in terms of reinterpreting or reworking the existing heritage. The literati heritage derived from the five Confucian classics, a collection of writings from the Zhou period that were believed to have been edited or composed by the Master himself. They comprised the *I Ching* or *Book of Changes*, which was used for divination; prescriptions for ritual and conduct; materials from which sprang the remarkable tradition of Chinese historical writing, described below; and *The Book of Songs*, the first known collection of Chinese poetry. Later on, the *Analects*, recording the sayings of Confucius, were incorporated along with various commentaries into the classics, which became the basis of the examination syllabus studied (or, to be more precise, memorized) by candidates for office.

The Book of Songs contains 305 poems, said to have been selected by Confucius himself and certainly used by him in his teaching; most of them probably date from the 9th to 7th centuries BC. So poetry was an ancient art; and it was also one that became closely linked with the imperial system. Its prestige was such that the common people revered it, and an emperor found nothing incongruous about reading his own verses aloud to encourage workers toiling on the canal system. As early as the Han period, literature was recognized as having a value independent of any moral or social message it might transmit, and literary fame was seen as an antidote to the oblivion inflicted by death. Educated persons habitually quoted poetry to one another, a practice encouraged by the examination system. Since the examinations also required candidates to compose verses, some facility in the art became almost universal among the literati, and over the centuries immense quantities of poetry were not only written but circulated in China.

Like most major forms of cultural expression, Chinese poetry was influenced by new developments and changes in fashion. Nevertheless it resembled the closely allied art of painting in displaying its creative variety within relatively narrow limits. Most verse was written in alternate rhyming lines of four, and later five or seven words. All the main verse-forms had been devised and exploited by the 10th century, and with certain important exceptions the typical Chinese poem had emerged as a brief lyric (usually four or eight lines), commemorating an event such as a meeting or parting, or expressing a personal emotion or a moment of revelation experienced during the contemplation of nature. These were events of a not unexpected kind in the life of a scholar-official, and, in particular, parting with beloved friends happened all too often in a career liable to entail postings to remote places; the most famous friends in Chinese history, the poets Bai Juyi and Yuan Zhen, were separated for years at a stretch, their meetings on occasion confined to a few hours when their boats met on the river while taking them in opposite directions on their official business.

Poets like these exchanged verses and wrote many of their works for a small circle of friends. Inevitably, many of them were highly allusive and, given their brevity, highly concentrated. But there were also very accessible works such as the popular ballads written by Bai Juyi, which were said to have been sung in tearooms as far afield as Korea and Japan. Bai (772–846) lived during the Tang era, generally considered to have produced the greatest flowering of Chinese poetry. Just before his time, three great writers were active:

The poet Wang Shizhen carrying a hoe. Despite his rustic activity here, Wang (1634–1711) combined a distinguished official career with the writing of sophisticated and highly allusive literary works.

the mystical nature poet Wang Wei (699–759) and the two giants of Chinese poetry, Li Bo (701–62) and Du Fu (712–70). Li Bo was unusual among poets in not pursuing an official career; wanderer, bohemian, drinker and Daoist, he has become the best-known Chinese writer to westerners, no doubt because of his life-style and reputed end, drowned in a barrel while drunkenly reaching for a reflection of the moon. But his greatness is unquestioned and was recognized by Du Fu, a more serious personality whose experiences of loss and exile intensified the nostalgic and melancholy quality of his writing.

China had a vigorous tradition of prose fiction in the form of short stories about the love affairs of emperors, scholars and courtesans, domestic troubles, magical journeys and the doings of ghosts and demons. Some of these were written during the Han period, and the genre was widely practised and admired under the Tang. From about the 14th century tales were written in the vernacular as well as in the classical literary language, a development that reflected a growing urban market for reading matter.

The same phenomenon probably accounts for the appearance of the first Chinese novels, which were also in the vernacular. However, they were not elaborations of the short story, but derived from the long-established tradition of oral story-telling as practised by professionals in market-places and similar public sites. By the Song period such performers were so proficient and abundantly provided with traditional or historical materials that their tale-telling took on a serial aspect, drawing customers day after day until a particular cycle had been completed. Written down, and sooner or later shaped by some editorial hand, these materials comprised the earliest novels. Significantly, even much later Chinese novels tended to resemble oral narratives in being episodic in construction and breaking off for interludes of poetry or song.

Popular historical traditions are embodied in two great early novels, filled with a relish for high adventure and derring-do that is reminiscent of Walter Scott or Dumas. *The Water Margin* concerns a group of 12th-century outlaws who made little impact on history but for some reason took

hold of the Chinese imagination; more and more feats and stratagems were attributed to them (as with Robin Hood, an even more obscure character whose historical existence is still unproven), and these provided the basis for *The Water Margin*. Adopting a now-familiar formula, the novel describes the adventures of each outlaw before bringing them all together under the leadership of Song Jiang, at first to defy the emperor but ultimately to serve him faithfully.

The Romance of the Three Kingdoms is based still more closely on recorded history, even quoting actual documents. It is set during the early 3rd century AD, when the Han empire was effectively extinct and the states of Wei, Wu and Shu were engaged in a struggle for supremacy. The novel combines heroic resolutions and bloody battles with political intrigues as the resourceful minister Zhuge Liang strives to save the small kingdom of Shu from the Machiavellian designs of the Wei warlord Cao Cao.

The ferocious conflicts that dominate *The Water Margin* and *The Romance of the Three Kingdoms* take on fantastic and comic forms in *The Journey to the West* (also known as *Monkey*). Unlike the earlier books, this 16th-century novel is attributed to a single author, Wu Chengen, but he undoubtedly drew on an existing mass of folktales that had accumulated around the central character and events. The narrative describes the arduous journey to India made by Xuanzang, the 7th-century monk who brought back and translated many authentic Buddhist texts. In Wu's version the monk is decidedly timid, and the adventure is carried forward by his escorts, especially a monkey and a pig whose magical powers do not prevent them from obeying their animal instincts at some inappropriate moments, with ridiculous or hair-raising consequences. Monkey, the best-equipped and most erratic of the pilgrims, finds himself at various times at war with heaven and locked in combat with a variety of monsters, but faithfully defends the Buddhist cause and is given his reward when the party finally returns to China with the precious texts.

The Golden Lotus also dates from the 16th century, but its author is unknown. Though based on an episode from *The Water Margin*, it is the

Opposite: the poet and his muse. *Zhen Hou Zhou and his Concubine seeking Inspiration for a Poem;* by an unknown artist of the school of Qin Ying, a leading 16th-century painter in the 'blue and green' style.

Above: an affecting moment in the play *The Western Chamber* as the scholar Chang parts with his beloved; the 14th-century text by Wang Shifu is illustrated here by two Ming artists, Wen Zhengmin and Qin Ying.

Opposite: word and image in harmony. In this hanging scroll, the poem, the picture (the Bodhi Buddha, with fan and prayer beads) and the space left unfilled are carefully balanced; ink and colour on paper.

first 'realist' Chinese novel: it chronicles the opulence and decline of a merchant household, focusing on private passions and domestic conflicts, money, and social and sexual relationships. Some critics consider it the greatest Chinese novel, but most have placed *The Story of the Stone* (also known as *The Dream of the Red Chamber/Red Mansions*) even higher. This extraordinary book is, among other things, the first Chinese work of fiction that is patently based on personal experience. Its author, Cao Xeqin, had a privileged childhood in a large and powerful Manchu family which was disgraced and ruined before he was fully grown up. After what seems to have been an obscure, erratic and alcoholic career, Cao Xeqin settled down in middle age to write, recreating the scenes of his childhood in the mansions of the fictional Jia family. The result was a novel of manners depicting the hurly-burly of a large aristocratic household and the changing fortunes of a very large cast of characters. But it is also a narrative of youthful experience and disillusion, moving from an enchanted garden to a harsh adult world of rivalries and deceit. *The Story of the Stone* is celebrated for its portraits of women; the central character, Jia Baoyu, is able to contemplate those of his own generation as a group of

'young girls in flower' and is given a poignant foreknowledge of their destinies; for the novel is also set, in a way that western readers find disconcerting, within a supernatural framework which intermittently shifts the narrative on to a different plane of existence. Cao Xeqin died in 1763 with his work still unfinished. A version was published in 1792, but a number of variant manuscripts exist (Cao appears to have made changes in deference to family objections), and these and other difficulties mean that no definitive text has ever been established. Current opinion is that Cao Xeqin wrote the first 80 of the 120 chapters, and that the morally satisfactory ending does not represent his own intention. But for Chinese readers this tangled literary tale only adds to the book's endless fascination.

Among other novels of note, written before Chinese literature was subjected to western influence, are *The Scholars* by Wu Jingzi (1701–1830), attacking the literati, and *Flowers in the Mirror* by Li Ruzhen (1763–1830), which denounces the oppression of women, notably through gender-reversal scenes in which a young male must undergo the agonies of footbinding and learn to become passive and compliant towards the dominant females.

Chinese authors wrote essays and memoirs, philosophical, religious, scientific and geographical works; but their achievements as historians were of particular note. It was perhaps their reverence for the past and tradition that made the Chinese so keenly aware of historical events and anxious to record and explain them. The earliest known historical works date from the Zhou period and belong to the Five Classics; the most important, *The Spring and Autumn Annals*, became the name by which the period 722–481 BC is still known. The doyen of Chinese historians was Sima Qian (c. 145–c. 86 BC) whose life work, *Historical Records*, covered the entire known past of China. Sima was so dedicated to his task that he allowed himself to suffer disgrace rather than abandon it. At court he made the mistake of defending a general who was out of favour, and as a result the Emperor Wudi sentenced the historian to be castrated. This was such a dishonour that a Chinese gentleman would normally have killed himself to avoid it; but Sima Qian 'submitted to the extreme penalty without rancour' in his determination to complete his manuscript.

The *Historical Records* is an encyclopaedic work, encompassing the annals of the ruling dynasties, chronological tables, monographs on subjects such as the economy, the calendar and religious and ceremonial practices, and biographical sketches of historical characters. A later historian, Ban Gu (AD 32–92), gave an even more wide-ranging account of the Han dynasty, and the works of Sima and Ban were taken as a model by later generations. One consequence was that a History Office was established under the Tang dynasty to collect and collate information about events as they occurred, with an eye to future use. From then onwards the officials of each dynasty compiled such records, doing so in the melancholy knowledge that they would be consulted only when the ruling family had forfeited the Mandate of Heaven and perished, enabling historians of the next dynasty to issue the 'standard history' of its predecessor. Though coloured by official Confucian values, these and other records have provided an account of imperial China that is unparalleled in its breadth, detail and documentation.

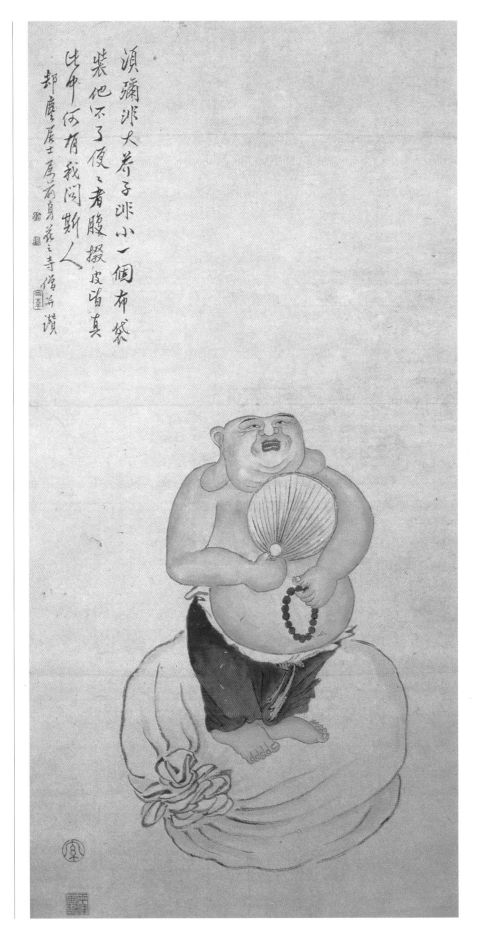

PERFORMING ARTS

Music was an essential element in Chinese life, ranging from worksongs to the hymns accompanying Confucian ceremonial. Inscriptions on Shang oracle bones (2nd millennium BC) demonstrate that flutes, drums, stone chimes (lithophones) and bells were already being played. Archaeological discoveries of the subsequent Zhou period included these and also mouth organs, pan pipes, and early versions of perhaps the most distinctive and admired of Chinese instruments, the zither. Confucius' statements emphasize the overwhelming emotional impact of music, and like the great Greek philosopher Plato he believed that its moral influence needed to be monitored, some modes being harmful because they encouraged luxurious or wanton thoughts. As in other cultures, song and poetry were closely related, and the early verses preserved in *The Book of Songs* may well have been selected by court musicians to make up a repertoire of lyrical, ceremonial and martial pieces on which they could draw at need.

By Han times, wealthy families also had musicians among their retainers, their stances in performance preserved in tomb decorations. Some instrumentalists were sufficiently well known by reputation to be imported for concerts given in the capital. Contacts with Central Asia led to the adoption of new instruments such as the lute and, under the Tang, the fiddle.

External pressures provoked a conservative cultural reaction among Chinese during the Song and Yuan periods, but the Mongol occupation did lead to one very important new development: the birth of the drama or, to describe it more accurately, the Chinese music-drama. Theatrical performances had certainly been a feature of life under the Song, especially in the big cities; but the content had been almost entirely music and dance, with little or no narrative element. This was only supplied when large numbers of literati found themselves unemployed by the conquering Mongols; they had previously rejected the idea of writing for money as beneath them, but in the

new circumstances many of them became willing to compose plays for the masses, even condescending to use the vernacular. Some of those who did so were remarkably industrious: about sixty titles by Guan Hanqing, probably the best-known of the Yuan dramatists, are on record, although only twenty survive.

Most Yuan plays are divided into four acts and alternate between spoken dialogue and songs. There is no doubt about the importance of these 'arias' in focusing the emotional significance of the scene, and it has often been suggested that 'opera' would be a better description of the form. (It was certainly the ancestor of the celebrated Beijing [Peking] Opera which developed in the 19th century and continues to be influential,

though its performances are not exactly operatic in the western sense.)

Nevertheless the narrative element in Yuan drama is important and effective, despite the anti-realistic conventions that prevailed. Some of these are usefully economical. Characters enter and simply inform the audience of their identities and intentions, and meetings and conflicts required by the plot are brought about instantly, with no preliminaries or plausible arrangements of circumstances. This stylization was emphasized by the costumes, which helped to identify the actor as belonging to a particular character-type, and by stock poses and movements that signalled actions and states of mind. The subjects of the plays included love stories, often with mythical or supernatural elements, and tales of injustice and revenge, usually set in the safely remote era of the Han. The popularity of revenge plays may have owed something to anti-Mongol feeling; at any rate, a number of plots involve the evil deeds of corrupt and ambitious military men, exposed and punished even though decades have passed since they were committed.

Despite the popularity of the drama, writing for the stage was never recognized as a serious literary occupation. Moreover, the vagabond, unconstrained life of the theatre was viewed with unease by the authorities. Actors were officially classed with prostitutes and their children and grandchildren were forbidden to present themselves as candidates for the civil service examinations. No respectable girl would go on the stage, and the actors who took female parts might be simultaneously celebrated for their talent and reviled for their assumed or actual homosexuality. Curiously, the low moral and social status of the theatrical profession in China had its exact counterpart in attitudes in many western countries down to the late 19th century.

Above: an animated pottery figure of an actor, made under the Yuan (Mongol) dynasty. It was during this period of alien rule that the first true Chinese dramas – amalgams of prose, verse and music – were composed and performed.

Left: musicians play for the party-loving Han Xicai: one of four scenes recording Han's *Night Entertainment* for a ruler who wanted to assess his suitability for office; 10th-century silk scroll by Gu Hongzhong.

6 CHINA AND THE WORLD

THE DISTINCTIVE AND ENDURING CHARACTER OF CHINESE CIVILIZATION IS OFTEN ATTRIBUTED TO ITS ISOLATION FROM OTHER CENTRES. MOUNTAINS, DESERTS, JUNGLES AND OCEANS HINDERED COMMUNICATIONS BETWEEN CHINA AND ALL BUT A HANDFUL OF SMALLER AND LESS ADVANCED SOCIETIES. THIS ISOLATION WAS NEVER COMPLETE: OVER THE CENTURIES, ASTRONOMICAL IDEAS FROM WESTERN ASIA, BUDDHISM FROM INDIA, AND CLOCKS, MISSIONARIES AND TRADERS FROM EUROPE WOULD CROSS THE MOUNTAINS, DESERTS, JUNGLES AND OCEANS. EVEN WHEN CHINA WAS LEAST ACCESSIBLE, MOBILE PEOPLES OF THE STEPPES AND NORTHERN FORESTS WOULD SERVE AS INTERMEDIARIES, CARRYING IDEAS, TECHNIQUES, STYLES OR OBJECTS BACKWARDS AND FORWARDS. HOWEVER, THESE OPERATIONS WERE SO SLOW AND INTERMITTENT THAT CHINA'S NATIVE CULTURE WAS NEVER OVERWHELMED, BUT THOROUGHLY ABSORBED AND NATURALIZED THE INFLUENCES THAT ARRIVED FROM BEYOND THE FRONTIERS. ONE CONSEQUENCE WAS THAT THE CHINESE CAME TO LOOK ON THEIR 'MIDDLE KINGDOM' AS TRULY THE CENTRE OF THE WORLD, MENACED AT TIMES BY UNRULY BARBARIANS BUT SO UNQUESTIONABLY SUPERIOR THAT EVEN THEIR ENEMIES IMITATED THEIR CULTURE AND WAY OF LIFE. THE COMPLACENCY BRED BY SUCH CONVICTIONS MADE THE HUMILIATIONS OF THE 19TH CENTURY ALL THE MORE DIFFICULT TO BEAR OR LEARN FROM. BUT THERE WERE CONSEQUENCES FOR OTHER CENTRES IN CHINA'S REMOTENESS: EXTRAORDINARY CHINESE FEATS OF DISCOVERY AND INVENTION, EVEN WHEN NOT DELIBERATELY KEPT SECRET, TOOK CENTURIES TO BECOME KNOWN AND MAKE AN IMPACT ON THE HISTORY OF THE WORLD AT LARGE.

SCIENCE AND TECHNOLOGY

Everybody knows that Chinese inventions such as paper, printing and gunpowder changed the course of human history, and that porcelain, lacquer and jade enlarged the repertoire of beautiful things. But many other advances were accomplished in workaday objects and practices, making the farmer's life less hard and his labour more productive. Most of these date from the last few centuries BC, during the turbulent Eastern Zhou and the stable, prosperous Han periods: surprisingly, the contrast between the two in political and public-order conditions seems to have had no appreciable effect on Chinese creativity. Iron ploughs enabled the farmer to drive deep furrows through the heaviest soil, which were neatly parted by efficient mould-boards. From the 3rd century BC ploughs and other tools were strengthened by being made of cast iron, a less brittle form of the metal which would remain unknown in Europe for many more centuries. Crops were planted in rows with seed-drills and regularly hoed to remove weeds, and after the harvest, winnowing (separating the grain from the chaff) was made speedier and simpler by an ingenious hand-turned fan mechanism that blew away the chaff while allowing the heavier grain to fall neatly into a box below.

By Han times, horses were equipped with trace-harnesses, so that when an animal pulled a load it took the pressure on to its chest rather than (as in the traditional harness used in both East and West) against its throat; and by the 5th century AD the trace-harness had been replaced by the even more efficient horse collar. Under the Han, the Chinese were also using the treadle-operated chain-pump for raising water, as well as

The Chinese art of paper-making: this late-18th-century painting shows pulped fibres being sieved so that the residue can be used to make sheets of paper. Large numbers of finished sheets are stacked on planks above the vat.

undertaking sophisticated hydraulic and engineering projects. Even more fundamental was the introduction of a single-wheeled vehicle for moving heavy loads – the wheelbarrow, one of those devices that appears to be obvious once it has been invented; nonetheless Europeans seem to have had nothing of the sort until a thousand years later. In fact all the innovations mentioned above were introduced by the Chinese at least several centuries before Europeans utilized them. Some may eventually have been discovered independently in the West, but it seems quite possible that the majority were based on information or ideas belatedly arriving from the Far East.

Knowledge of paper and printing also spread very slowly. By the 5th century paper was the standard writing material in China, and was also employed for such Chinese innovations as kites and toilet paper. One 9th-century Arab commentator described their use of the latter with disgust, denouncing it as an unsanitary substitute for washing; but by then the Arabs were themselves making paper (for writing on, at any rate) and

finding a market for it further west. Arab commercial policy may have prevented the secret of paper-making from reaching Europe for a time, but the fact that the first paper-mills were not set up until 1270 (at Fabriano in Italy) suggests that more profound cultural or economic factors were at work. An economist might point to the absence of a sufficiently large, adequately affluent and literate market; a cultural historian might place more emphasis on the traditionalism, the clerical elitism, and even the heavenward-orientation of the European Middle Ages. In China, at least seven centuries separated the invention of paper from the introduction of printing, so a maturation of European society does seem to be discernible in the relatively small time that elapsed between the founding of the Fabriano works and Gutenberg's use of movable type in the 1450s. The revolutionary effects of these developments hardly needs to be stressed; to give just a single example, not much more than a half-century after Gutenberg, the printing of Martin Luther's writings gave Protestant ideas a swift, European-wide

A farmer ploughing in 1874. The scene is apparently age-old, but in fact Chinese agriculture underwent radical technological changes, enabling the country to support its huge population.

currency, transforming what would previously have been a scholar's dissent or localized heresy into a crisis which fractured Western Christendom and in doing so released a host of powerful new forces.

The intense contacts occasioned by wars often lead to a rapid transmission of new techniques and ideas. The Chinese invention of the stirrup, probably in the 3rd century AD, greatly enhanced the role of the mounted warrior. (There were advantages for civilians too, of course, but of a less spectacular kind.) Locked into his steed, he could travel faster, negotiate rough terrain more securely, and bear a far greater weight of arms and armour without any danger of becoming unbalanced and unhorsed; had the stirrup not been invented, the knight-in-armour of famous quests and crusades would never have existed. A fierce steppe people, the Avars, copied the stirrups of the Chinese and, heading west in the 6th century, so harassed and impressed the Byzantines that they quickly followed suit. Viking mercenaries in the pay of the Byzantines brought the stirrup to

Above: horse and carriage: the horse is wearing a collar harness, taking the pressure on its chest. When this watercolour was painted, c.1800, the Chinese had been using such collars for some 2,000 years.

Left: one of the earliest surviving stirrups, made of bronze in China during the 6th or 7th century AD. This simple yet revolutionary device greatly influenced war and travel.

western Europe, but this proved to be another innovation whose time had not yet come, almost certainly because western smiths had not developed the necessary skills to cast bronze or iron. The formidable 'knights in armour' of popular tales only appeared in any numbers early in the Middle Ages, when troubadours and trouvères soon began to transform them into heroes of ancient romance, performing great deeds in some long-vanished golden age of chivalry. The reality, however, was the emergence of a new, tank-like war-weapon that would prove near-irresistible for centuries to come.

The Chinese made other significant contributions to the military arts, notably the crossbow. By the Zhou period this was a highly efficient weapon with a precision-made bronze trigger; eventually rapid-fire and artillery-size versions were developed, equipped with poison-tipped bolts. But the most far-reaching development was the invention of gunpowder and its employment in the earliest guns; contrary to a widespread belief, the Chinese were not content to exploit the properties of the new substance by making harmless firecrackers, but used it as a war-weapon in the 10th century, probably a few decades after its discovery. In the 11th century its manufacture became a government monopoly; its value – and dangers – were evidently realized, since the export of the main ingredients, saltpetre (potassium nitrate) and sulphur, was prohibited. Grenades, bombs and rockets were devised, increasingly destructive as the Chinese discovered the proportions of saltpetre, sulphur and charcoal required to create explosions that could shatter metal casings and propel the fragments in all directions. At the same time, primitive guns were fashioned that functioned rather like flame-throwers, flinging out jets of fire through bamboo tubes. From these the Chinese progressed to true metal hand-guns and artillery (such as 'the long-range, awe-inspiring cannon'), grouped in batteries to inflict heavy casualties on an incautious foe. How effective they were in practice is not certain, since many extant battle descriptions are of glorious victories by the Jin or Chinese over the Mongols – who, however, conquered both peoples. It was certainly European experience that guns and gunpowder had only a small influence on the outcome of wars for several centuries after their introduction. The earliest evidence for the use of cannon in Western Europe comes from mid-13th-century Spain, and the actual formula for gunpowder appears in the writings of the contemporary English scientist Roger Bacon; but it seems unlikely that any European battle was decided by firearms or artillery before the late 15th century. This date, of course, does not alter the fact that the development of firearms, artillery and explosives constituted an unarguably world-changing, if problematic, Chinese achievement.

Of the many other Chinese scientific discoveries and inventions, perhaps the most impressive concerned ships and navigation. The Chinese are not generally thought of as a seafaring people, no doubt because their vessels and weaponry were patently inferior to the West when the first serious naval clashes occurred in the 19th century. But riverborne traffic and coastal trade were important in their earlier history; the Chinese

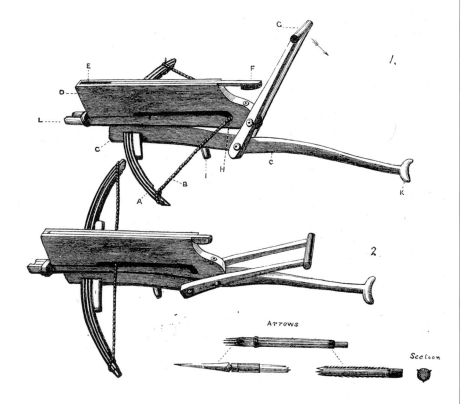

Deadly weapon: as developed by the Chinese, the 'machine gun' crossbow incorporated a magazine which made it possible for a soldier to fire something like an arrow every second. Though only effective at short range, it was devastating against mass attacks.

Direction finder: a 19th-century Chinese mariners' compass of traditional type. The magnetic properties of the lodestone were known from a very early date, and Europeans may well have learned the navigational use of the compass from the Chinese.

replaced the Arabs as seaborne carriers under the Song; and Zheng He's 15th-century expeditions from side to side of the Indian Ocean were conducted on a greater scale than anything that contemporary Europeans dared to contemplate. Indeed, historians enjoy speculating about what would have happened if the Ming had not decided to turn their backs on the world and the little Portuguese ships of Vasco da Gama had reached India in 1498 to find gigantic junks such as Zheng He's in its harbours.

Most of the advanced features of junks have already been mentioned, but it is worth pointing out that both the rudder and the compass were known to the Chinese at a remarkably early date. An existing pottery model of a ship with a rudder has been dated to the 1st century AD. The mag-

netic properties of the lodestone were known even earlier, but for centuries it was used primarily for determining the correct alignment of buildings and graves (feng-shui). Somewhere between 850 and 1050 – significantly, at a time when long-distance commerce was flourishing under the Song – Chinese ships began to carry a compass to help them navigate during murky weather, when there was no help to be had from the sun or the stars. Neither the rudder nor the compass appears to have been used by Europeans before the 12th century. Whether they were independently discovered or learned from the Chinese via intermediaries is not clear, but without them, the 15th-century voyages of discovery and the great extension of European power would certainly not have happened.

Coment les .ij. freres vindrent au grant kaan.
Quant les deux freres furent venus au grant kaan il les
...

The Polos welcomed by the Great Khan: one of many similar late medieval manuscript illuminations, painted to accompany accounts of the fabulous East by Marco Polo and other explorers.

JOURNEYS WITHIN AND WITHOUT

China is such a vast and geographically varied land that journeys within its present-day borders can still be formidable undertakings. In the past, large numbers of Chinese travelled as colonists (for example, from the North to the lands south of the Yangtze), and conscript soldiers and convict labourers were often marched from one end of the Middle Kingdom to another. Even so, some provinces remained little known, and as late as the 17th century a classic book of travel was written by the monk Xu Xiake, who penetrated the mountain country of Yunnan in the south-west, an area still regarded as remote and mysterious some two hundred and fifty years after its incorporation into Ming China.

For centuries the Chinese were unaware of the existence of people like themselves, settled and organized into complex, literate, city-building societies ('civilizations'). This fact graphically illustrates China's isolation, and largely explains the Chinese sense of living at the centre of the world and being unquestionably superior to the barbarians around them. Since the barbarians, however inferior, were also dangerous, information about them was useful, and no doubt spies, scouts and merchants made many journeys into the 'Outer Regions' of which we know nothing. The first Chinese traveller-explorer on record was Zhang Qian. He was despatched in 138 BC to contact and, if possible, make an alliance with the

Yuezhi, a tribe somewhere in the west who were known to be bitterly hostile to the Xiongnu, the current menace to China's frontiers. Zhang Qian's extraordinary adventures began when he was captured by the Xiongnu, who provided him with a wife and kept him captive for ten years. After he managed to escape, Zhang simply went on with his mission, found the Yuezhi in Bactria (modern Afghanistan), but failed to convince their chief that it was worth reviving an old quarrel when there were richer pickings to the west.

On his way back, Zhang spent another year as a prisoner of the Xiongnu before arriving at Changan in 126 BC. Though the political objective of his mission had not been achieved, he brought back quantities of useful information, including news of other states – Central Asian Ferghana and its big horses, Parthia still further west, and a land where elephants were used in battle – India – to the south-east of Bactria. Realizing that such a land must be relatively near, the Chinese emperor sent an expedition to reach it overland by a south-westerly route, but the natural and human obstacles in this direction were too great, under the Han and for long afterwards.

Zhang Qian led a further embassy to Central Asia, and in time his success in extending Chinese influence was followed by commercial relations and the opening up of the Silk Road. Although goods generally passed from hand to hand along the Road, in 106 BC one Chinese caravan did travel all the way to Persia; but this was almost the furthest extent of westward land exploration before modern times. One intrepid envoy, Gan Yin, did journey even further, possibly reaching the Syrian coast in AD 97; apparently bound for Rome, he gave up after being told (wrongly) that there were still months or years of travel ahead of him. Consequently Han China and the Roman Empire rose and fell, meanwhile exchanging goods, without ever acquiring any certain knowledge of each other.

India also remained unreached, despite Zhang Qian's report. But the growth of Buddhism in China created a wish to visit the shrines associated with the Enlightened One, and to obtain authentic copies of religious texts. The first recorded pilgrim was a monk named Fa Xian, who left Changan in 339, followed the Silk Road as far as the Pamirs, and then went down into India through the north-west passes. He arrived after a five-year trip and then spent six years studying and visiting shrines before making his way back to China by sea.

Fa's account of his experiences emphasizes the dangers of the journey (throwing in some very tall tales for good measure), but describes India itself as peaceful and prosperous. This was no longer the case when a more important scholar, Xuanzang, or Tripitaka, made the journey in 629–45; his abrupt changes of fortune, and his ultimate triumph in returning with quantities of manuscripts and relics, made him a popular hero whose ever-more-exaggerated exploits were finally written down in novel form as *The Journey to the West*. Despite unstable conditions in India, where Buddhists were sometimes harshly treated, large numbers of Chinese pilgrims subsequently made

An empire unveiled: early-18th-century map of China and Japan, published in London by Hermann Moll. Western attention was increasingly concentrated on the wonders – and the weaknesses – of the Celestial Empire.

the journey. But instead of taking the arduous Central Asian route, most of them went by sea via the Indonesian islands, often stopping off in Sumatra to study Sanskrit so that they could read Buddhist scriptures in the original.

These Chinese travellers were transported by foreign vessels. But under the Song the Chinese became seafarers, and for a few hundred years they made long voyages culminating in Zheng He's great transoceanic journeys; it has been claimed that during this period they rounded the Cape of Good Hope and sighted Australia. The decision to abandon such expeditions and destroy all of Zheng He's records heralded a turning-away from the outside world by the Ming which was maintained by the Qing, despite their own foreign origin. At best, an emperor would display a benevolent interest in the habits and ingenious inventions of foreigners, if they took the trouble to come to China; and Chinese scholars were open-minded enough to learn from their European visitors and make significant advances in mathematics and cartography.

In the 19th century the Chinese again became great travellers, but in radically different circumstances from anything in the past. A few went abroad to study western science and technology; huge numbers left in search of a better life (without necessarily finding it), settling in South-East Asia, Oceania, the Americas and other lands.

The exertions required of early Chinese travellers to reach foreign lands were equally unavoidable by those who came to the Middle Kingdom. One possible exception was the merchant able to take advantage of the Arab mastery of the sea. From the 8th century to the 10th, Canton was a cosmopolitan port with many Muslim residents, and the merchant Suleyman (already quoted on the subject of porcelain) left a description of life in the city shortly before it was sacked by the rebel Huang Chao in 879.

The rarity of writings by non-Chinese travellers reflects the medieval attitude to such things (more interested in marvels than factual accounts), and in particular the observations of generations of far-ranging merchants perished with them. We possess Marco Polo's *Description of the World* only through the double accident that cast him into a Genoese prison and put him in touch with a professional writer hungry for copy. And Polo and other Europeans were only able to reach China because the cruel Mongol leader Genghis Khan had destroyed all the great and petty rulers across Asia whose wars and oppressions hindered trade and travel; for a brief period both became possible thanks to the 'Mongol Peace' (Pax Mongolica) obtaining from end to end of the continent.

Most of those who crossed Asia and left accounts of their travels hoped to convert the Great Khan to Christianity, incidentally saving Europe from an invasion that it seemed ill-equipped to repel. (Fortunately for Europe the invasion never materialized, despite the spiritual obstinacy of the Khans.) Friar Giovanni de Plano Carpini (1225–47) and Friar Guillaume de Rubrouk (1247–54) both made the journey, and Guillaume wrote a heartfelt account of the miseries endured, the opulent savagery of the Mongol way of life and the jealousies and intrigues of rival missionaries. But neither of the friars travelled beyond the Mongolian capital of Karakorum. The first visitors to Beijing, and China proper, arrived there in the 1260s, almost by accident. The brothers Maffeo and Niccolo Polo had intended to return to their native Venice after trading on the Volga, but made a long detour in order to avoid a war zone. At Bukhara in Central Asia they encountered a Mongol official who told them that they would receive a warm and profitable reception at the court of the Great Khan. The brothers were convinced and went on to 'Cambaluc' (Beijing), the Chinese capital of Kublai Khan. More urbane and curious than his predecessors, Kublai received the visitors with enthusiasm and eventually dispatched them with a letter to the pope, asking him to send learned men who could describe and debate the merits of Christianity.

The Polos returned to Europe, carried out their mission and then began their second long journey to Cambaluc in 1271. The friars sent with them by the pope were frightened off by dangers on the way, but the brothers reached their destination in 1275, this time accompanied by Niccolo's son Marco (1254–1324). Kublai was now effectively master of China, and the Polos benefited from the

Mongol policy of employing foreigners. By his own account, the young Marco became a great favourite with the emperor, travelling through China on special missions and finally being appointed governor of Yangzhou. In 1292, after they had spent seventeen years in his service, Kublai reluctantly agreed to allow the Polos to leave, as the escorts of a Mongol princess bound for Persia. After delivering her safely they returned to Venice in 1295.

Now a leading citizen, Marco commanded a galley in a war between Venice and Genoa. Captured, he passed his time by dictating the story of his experiences to his fellow-prisoner, Rustichello. As a professional, Rustichello 'improved' the material, among other things inserting passages from his own earlier writings. This may have helped to give *The Description of the World* its vogue in a Europe mainly interested in tales of the marvellous, but it has since made it difficult to distinguish between genuine, hearsay

Opposite: Chinese workers in 1866, using a snow plough during the building of the Union Pacific Railroad, USA. In the 19th and 20th centuries Chinese settled in the USA, Malaysia, Indonesia, Fiji and many other places.

Below: Jean Joseph Amiot (1718–93), a French Jesuit missionary who spent most of his life in China. Favoured by the Emperor Qianlong, he wrote many works introducing Chinese history, art and thought to the West.

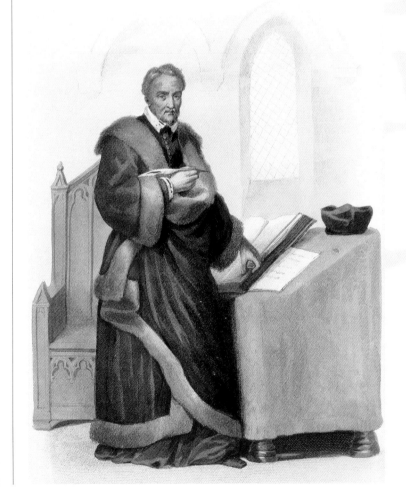

Wallpaper in pseudo-Chinese style; it was presented to Coutts the bankers by Lord Macartney, leader of the first British embassy to China. Such fanciful chinoiserie was immensely popular in 18th-century Europe.

and imaginary material in the book. There is also a strong possibility that Marco may have drawn heavily on the experiences of his father and uncle (it has even been suggested that he may not have travelled any further than the family's trading post in the Crimea). However, despite all of these problems there is little doubt that the *Description* contains a solid core of information, all the more valuable in that Kublai's death in 1295 ended the already intermittent Mongol Peace and closed the

Silk Road. A few intrepid individuals subsequently managed to reach China from Europe, notably Friar Odoric of Pordenone in 1327, who showed a more lively interest than the materialistic Marco in unusual customs such as foot-binding and fishing with cormorants. But essentially China and Europe again lost touch without deeply influencing each other. Paradoxically, during this very period, under the Yuan and early Ming dynasties, China developed commercial and

European perceptions of China were initially shaped by the desirability of Chinese products and the reports of Jesuit missionaries who admired the Confucian official class. The result was that for most of the 18th century, writers such as Voltaire were able to make satirical points by comparing the supposedly rational and humane Chinese order with the injustice and unreason that prevailed in their own society.

But irritation with Chinese aloofness and an appreciation of Chinese weakness soon became apparent. As early as Lord Macartney's embassy in 1793, the non-meeting of minds was complete. Rejecting any possibility of a relationship, Qianlong informed George III that he had made allowances for him: 'I do not forget the lonely remoteness of your island, cut off from the world by intervening wastes of sea.' More realistically, Macartney described China as 'an old, crazy, first-rate man-of-war, which a fortunate succession of able and vigilant officers has continued to keep afloat . . . and to overawe their neighbours merely by her bulk and appearance'. These two statements provide the keys to many 19th-century disasters, and anticipate the climax: the possibly inevitable but also self-inflicted death of China's ancient imperial order.

Blue-and-white 'willow pattern' dish made by a pottery in Devon. Illustrating a 'Chinese' tale that is a purely Western invention, willow-pattern ware is a classic example of Europe constructing its own, imaginary East.

diplomatic relations with most of the states of Asia, and Chinese seafarers were making their most extensive voyages.

Among the visitors from distant lands was the great Moroccan traveller Ibn Battuta, whose incredible wanderings took him to India and then, in 1346, on to China, where he too noted the existence of such wonders as porcelain and paper money. The arrival of Europeans by sea and its consequences have been described earlier.

INDEX